Drawing

The Beginners Manual

Drawing

The Beginners Manual

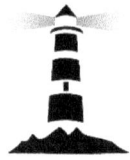

© Copyright 2015 Lighthouse Press

This document is geared towards providing exact and reliable information in regards to the topic and issue covered. The publication is sold with the idea that the publisher is not required to render accounting, officially permitted, or otherwise, qualified services. If advice is necessary, legal or professional, a practiced individual in the profession should be ordered.

- From a Declaration of Principles which was accepted and approved equally by a Committee of the American Bar Association and a Committee of Publishers and Associations.

Table of Contents

Introduction

A lot of psychologists and therapists across the globe have become enamored with the idea of Zentangle. First created by a husband and wife team, Zentangle took hold because it's a basic, simple concept that allows anyone, even young children, to participate. The read psychologists and therapist have become interested in the technique of drawing within a small tangle, or a closed line, is due to the benefits.

Zentangle has been shown to help treat many different ailments such as depression, anxiety, stress, schizophrenia, and many other mental illnesses. However, you don't have to be suffering from one of these illnesses to enjoy the benefits of Zentangle. Just about anyone in the modern world has doodled on a piece of paper, but Zentangle is much more than that. It's taking that focus and honing it in on what you're doing, and living in the present moment.

Many of us have forgotten how to do that, but I'm going to show you how to live in the present again with some simple steps. I hope you enjoy the journey! I know that you can become a Zentangle expert in no time with these easy to follow steps!

Chapter One – The Benefits of Zentangle

When Zentangle was first introduced to the world, it was meant to be used to help people relax and calm their minds, protecting them from the daily stresses of life. Since then, Zentangle has been studied by psychologists across the globe for its different beneficial aspects. Before you start your adventure into Zentangle, let's first discuss what it's for so that you understand the instructions you'll find later in this book. My job is to make you an expert on Zentangle, and you first have to understand what it's all about before you start putting pen to paper!

Psychological Benefits

There are many different psychological benefits to Zentangle. In fact, it's not being used by therapists and psychologists alike to help their patients feel calmer and more relaxed during their sessions. They're also encouraged to continue the practice during their ordinary lives to bring about that feeling of inner peace and harmony.

Let's take a look at the psychological benefits in more detail.

- **Relaxation.** Zentangle is currently being used as a lighthearted way to help people unwind from their stresses of the day. It draws in their focus by drawing them away from the agitation subtly. The intricate, deliberate strokes lead to something beautiful and unique, thus making the artist feel at peace.

- **Relieve Stress.** The pressures of the day seem to lift away when the artist is drawing their Zentangle. The enlightening, liberating movements ease away the tension. This makes it perfect for those who are engaging in a stressful meeting within moments and need to relax, or those who need to clear their head before they talk to someone about a complication.

- **Improve Self-Esteem.** It feels like an accomplishment to complete a Zentangle. Patients and artists like to see their Zentangle come to fruition, allowing them a sense of pride and accomplishment.

- **Therapy.** Those who are suffering from a medical condition or a mental condition will benefit from completing Zentangle because they are able to focus less on their condition and more on what they are accomplishing in the present.

- **Anger Management.** Those who suffer from anger management will greatly benefit from Zentangle as it helps them take their mind off what they were upset about and allows them to focus on that feeling of peace and calmness.

- **Addiction Therapy.** Those who suffer from addiction may find Zentangle to be a great relief because they are able to focus less on the cravings and the stress of daily life, and focus more on completing their design. Addiction is a powerful thing, but Zentangle can be even more powerful.

- **Attention Deficit Disorder.** One of the more important aspects of Zentangle is that it allows the person performing it to focus. It forces them to hone in on their concentration skills and keeps them engaging in the flow of creation. While it ultimately relaxes that person, Zentangle is easier and easier over time, allowing for a sort of relaxed focus.

Physical Benefits

Just as there are many psychological benefits to Zentangle, there are many physical benefits as well. Zentangle has been used for stroke patients, amputees, and for those who need to improve their sleep. Let's take a look at some of these and more in finer detail.

- **Improved Sleep Patterns.** Zentangle has been proven to help those who are suffering from abnormal sleep patterns, such as sleeping during the day or not being able to sleep at night, realign their sleep patterns so that they're normal again. It works by helping them relax, focus, and allowing the mind to sort out its complications from the day while the person is still awake. This allows the brain to power down at the end of the day due to the worries of the day's stresses already having been dealt with.

- **Improved Hand-Eye Coordination.** Those who have suffered from an accident or medical illnesses that impair their hand-eye coordination can benefit from doing Zentangle. While it's simple and easy to do, it forces the artist to focus on the lines that they're drawing, thus improving their motor skills.

- **Develop Fine Motor Skills.** Those who have suffered a stroke or another ailment are now being instructed to do Zentangle in order to not only help their hand-eye coordination, but to fine tune their damaged motor skills.

Other Benefits

While there are some great psychological and physical benefits to Zentangle, there are numerous more. Take a peek at these benefits and see if you couldn't benefit at least one way from Zentangle!

- **Develop and Nurture Creative Abilities.** For those who suffer from feeling that you're never creative, Zentangle is a great way to get into that vibe and to really maximize that side of your life. Your mind will frolic and grow in ways that you never thought were possible before.

- **Journal Prompting.** For those who are seeing a psychologist or would just like to write down their thoughts and emotions into a journal, Zentangle is a good way to bring about those thoughts and emotions from the day. It allows the mind to rest and view the day's events from afar.

- **Creates Amazing Art.** Zentangle is something that no one can fail. It brings about the innermost emotions and thoughts of the person creating it and truly represents their personality. Therefore, the art that is created with Zentangle is always beautiful.

- **Helps with Team Building and Group Focus.** While an amazing piece can be created on your own, Zentangle actually is an excellent idea for a group activity. It helps connect many minds together so that they can bond and get to know one another through their art.

- **Home Schooling.** Students who are home-schooled are now getting into Zentangle because it helps them focus before their classes and before they do an assignment. It helps their minds get into the zone of learning.

- **Design Inspiration.** Zentangle is art at its very core. Just as any other form, it has themes from both external and internal forces. These forces come together to form a design structure that has the power to inspire artists to create something even more complex and beautiful.

- **Self-Soothing.** When you're accomplishing something that is repetitive and creative at the same time, it can be very soothing for the mind and the soul. Some research on Zentangle has suggested that the engagement in this process has relaxation benefits, and this I particularly true if you go into the process without any expectations other than enjoyment.

- **It's Simple.** All you really need is a piece of paper and a pen in order to create Zentangle, so anyone who can get a hold of those two materials can do it!

- **It Teaches You to Own Mistakes.** When you use a pen on paper, it requires that you take the risk of making mistakes. Most Zentangle art has some sort of mistake in it that can't be erased, so it teaches you how to incorporate what may seem like a mistake into the completed piece of art. It's a great metaphor for your daily life. Nothing is perfect and how you adjust to those imperfections is what really matters.

- **Reinforces Aimlessness.** In a day and age when we focus only on our preplanned day, we tend to forget about being spontaneous and aimless. Zentangle teaches you to be that person again. It teaches you how to accept what has happened in the past, teaches you how to perform mindlessness, and how to go with the flow of the future. Zentangle teaches children and adults alike not to always strive for number one, but to strive for what's best for you. When we're focused on the past or the future, we tend to forget about the present and we miss out on a lot of adventures and experiences. But if you are able to sit down and draw a Zentangle without thinking about how long it's taking you, when it'll be done, and what you'll be doing after you're finished, you've mastered mindlessness. It's all about living in the moment, and Zentangle can teach you that.

- **Entertainment.** For those who are looking for an alternative form of relaxing entertainment, Zentangle is a good choice. You can do this either alone or with a group. Imagine your friends sitting down in a circle and drawing their Zentangles. It'd be a quiet, relaxing moment between people who respected and loved one another.

There are many more benefits of Zentangle that are just waiting to be discovered. I hope that you can discover unique benefits to you as you perform the art of Zentangle, but first, you must know what you'll need in order to get started. Let's take a look at materials you may want to gather before you start your adventure into the Zentangle world!

Chapter Two – Materials Needed

There are very few supplies that are really needed for Zentangle, and depending on which type you'll be performing, you'll need different supplies. First, we're going to look at the supplies needed for the original form of Zentangle, and then we'll take a look at some of the more unconventional supplies and ideas that people have used over the years. You're going to become a Zentangle expert in no time!

Original Zentangle Materials

When Zentangle was first introduced to the world, it was introduced with the idea that all you needed was a three-inch by three-inch piece of heavy duty white paper and a fine tipped black pen. So if you truly want to get into the spirit of the original version of Zentangle, grab yourself a black pen with a nice, felt tip and a piece of white paper that is heavy enough it will withstand the test of time.

Unconventional Supplies and Ideas

When it comes to paper, you don't necessarily have to have paper. Some have Zentangled on dominos, take out coffee cups, napkins, newspapers, their hands, in a journal, on an old envelope, and on a sticky note. So you don't have to stick with just paper, plus you have the opportunity to Zentangle more often if you're not just limited to paper.

In addition, when you choose a pen for Zentangling, most people would go for the fine tipped, black pen. Fine tipped pens do allow you to create an intricate, detailed design, but they're not always as fun! Some have chosen to use crayons, colored pencils, colored pens, and even paint to make their Zentangle really stand out! So if you want to go with the original design, use a fine tipped black pen, but if you feel a little more out of the box than most, go for something with color.

In addition to pens being used, pencils are often used by Zentanglers to shade in strings and sections of their Zentangle to make it really stand out and give it depth. So if you're someone who has a creative, artistic side, then go for getting a pencil and doing a little shading! If you want to keep your Zentangle from smudging after you've shaded it, use a little acrylic spray to spritz it. It'll keep all the colors and shading from running together if people handle it!

The moral of this chapter is that while you should start out with original Zentangle materials, you can branch out into any form that you would like in the future. The options are literally limitless! Now that you know what you need let's take a look at how you can get started with your first attempt at Zentangle.

Chapter Three – Zentangling and First Attempts

For your first attempt at Zentangle, you should probably start off with the original version of this practice. After that, we'll get into some more details about different patterns and how to branch out to different platforms in later chapters. But for now, let's start off with a description of the materials you'll need for this exercise so that you can enjoy Zentangle the right way!

Step One – Supplies

The original method of Zentangle instructs the student to purchase some fine printmaking paper that's of sturdy material. You can use a sturdy piece of white construction paper that you cut to a 3 ½" square. Just as long as it's the proper size and the proper color, you should be okay.

You'll then need a pen with a very fine tip that's black. We'll get into using colors later on, but you want to get an idea of the pattern before you start adding colors to them.

An example of a pen that you might use could be a Sharpie Pen with a felt tip. The ones shown below are retractable and convenient for Zentangling wherever you may be.

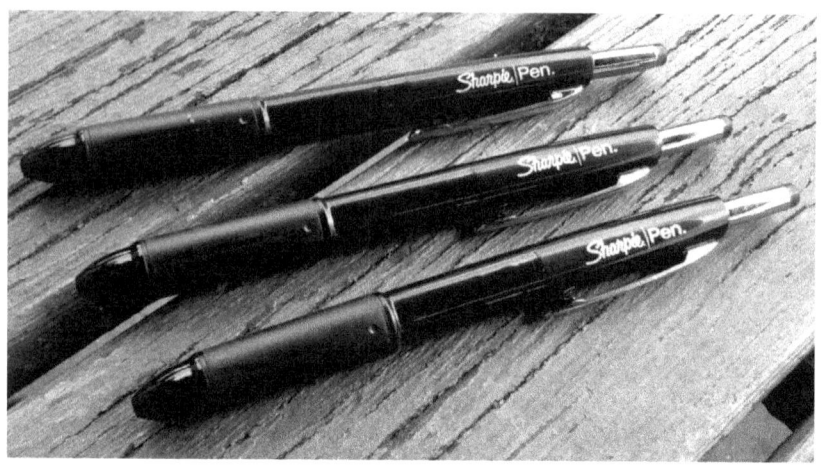

Photo courtesy of redspotted at Flickr.com

Step Two – Draw Your Border

Once you have the supplies, you'll then need to use a pencil to create a border. Draw a very light square border around the edge of the piece of paper. The pattern you draw will be within the perimeter of this border. You should not use a ruler or a straight edge to draw the border! Just freehand sketch it near the edges of the paper.

It's fine if your hand has wavered while you drew the border. It'll be unique and original then, and the pattern will emerge within the original confines. If it looks uneven or has wavy lines, the finished piece is going to be that much more original than someone else's.

You should not press down hard with the pencil and should freehand the border. It's not meant to be visible once the Zentangle is completed with the pen.

Photo courtesy of Author

Step Three – Draw the String

Once you have the border drawn with the pencil, you'll then want to draw a string inside the border. A string is a curved line or a squiggle that is going to create the structure of the design. The pattern that you make is going to come about due to the contours of that string. It should be very lightly sketched with the pencil, abstract, simple, and divides the border into different sections.

You should not press down hard with the pencil when you draw the string. It's not going to be visible once the Zentangle pattern is finished because it's just meant to serve as a guideline for the pattern.

Some find it hard to figure out how they're going to draw the string. Remember that the Zentangle should be a pleasurable experience and that it should feel natural. Draw whatever comes to your mind when you put the pencil to the paper. There is no wrong way to draw your string!

Photo courtesy of Author

Step Four – Create the Tangle

Once you have the border and the string drawn, you can begin to create your tangle. The tangle is the actual pattern that arises from the string. You should be using the pen at this point. A Zentangle can have more than one tangle, so go with however you'd like to create it. There is no right or wrong when it comes to a Zentangle. When you're working on it, keep some of these tips in mind.

- Tangles should be made of simple shapes like lines, dots, circles, and squiggles.
- Penciled shading is able to be added when you're finished, but skip this until you're completely done with the Zentangle.

Let's take a look at how to create a tangle from the string I created above.

Step A

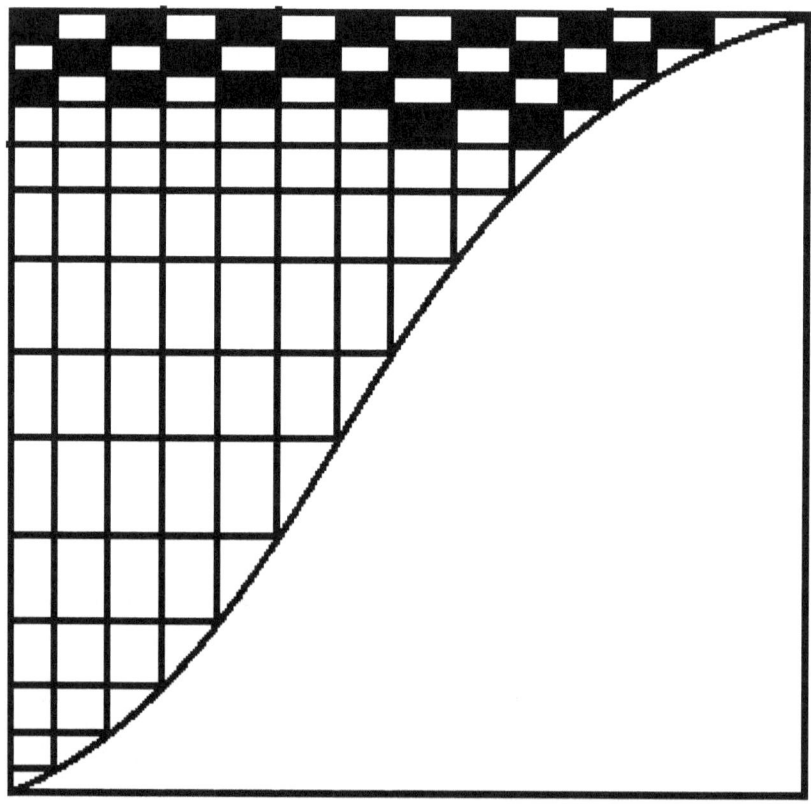

Photo courtesy of Author

As you can see, I started a checkerboard pattern on the left hand side off the string and began to fill in every other block to give it a checkerboard appearance.

Step B

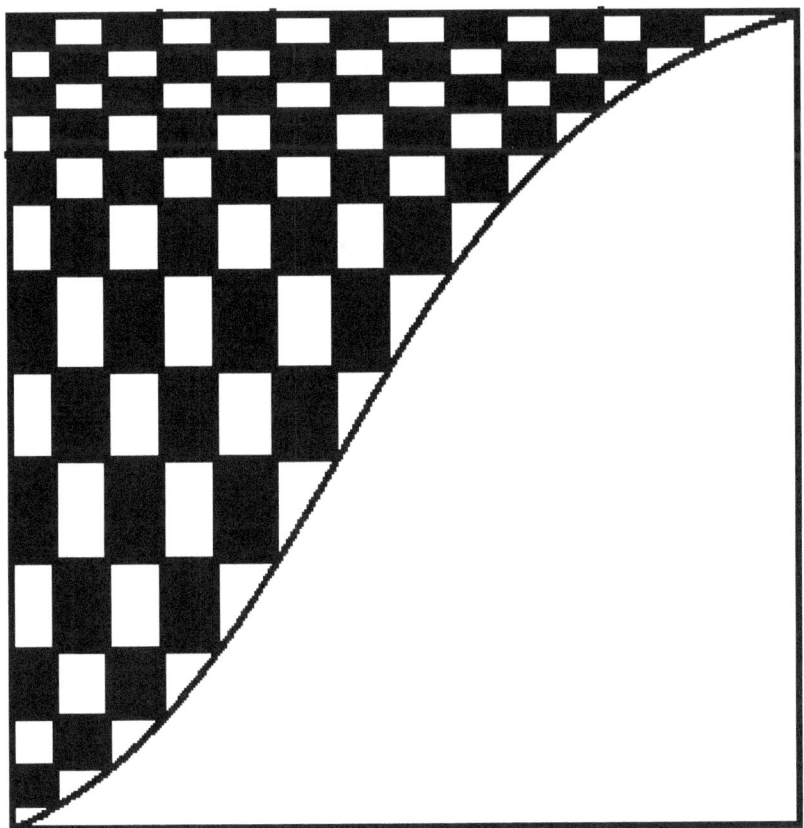

Photo courtesy of Author

I'm now finished with the checkerboard pattern on the left side and finished with shading. I'm going to put in a ray pattern on the right side to finish it all off with a little shading, like so.

Step C

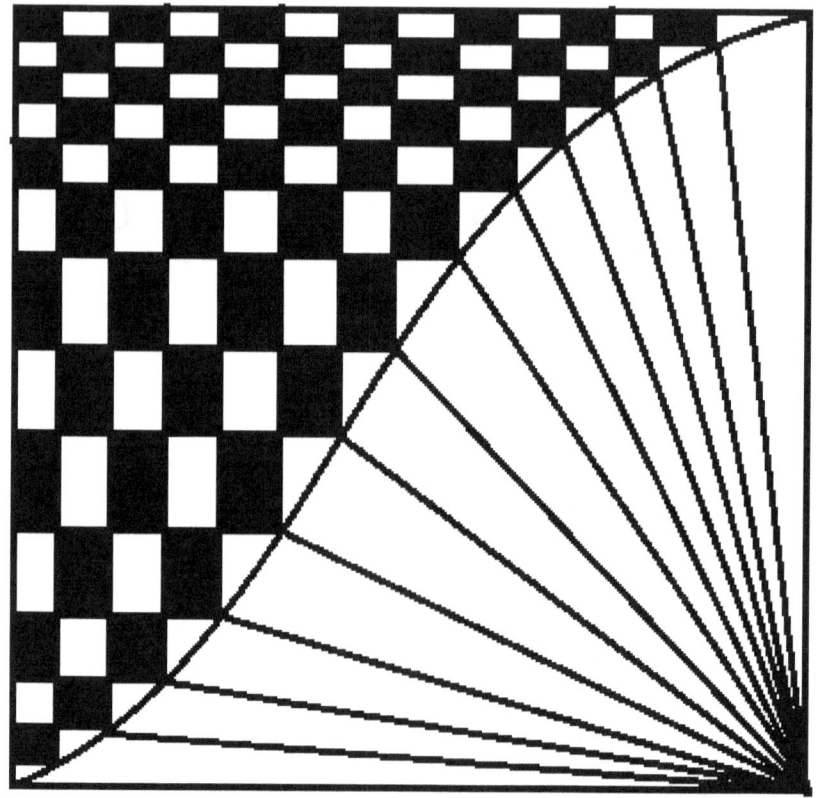

Photo courtesy of Author

And now for the shading:

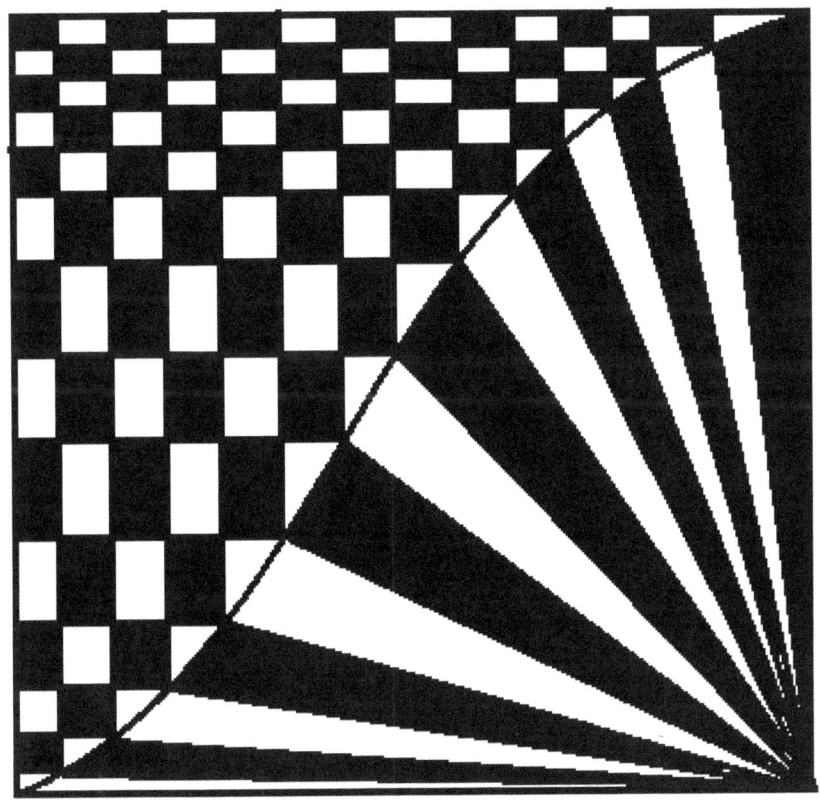

Photo courtesy of Author

As you can see in the previous Zentangle shown, there are obvious lines where the tangle was drawn, but the two patterns seem to complement one another.

Step Five – Never Erase

When you're working with pen, you're not going to be able to erase neatly, and that's part of the reason the Zentangle is created with a pen and not a pencil. There is no going back when you create one of these. Every Zentangle is built with your precise strokes, and paying attention to those strokes is what helps you keep your mind focused and relaxed at the same time. Focus intently on the Zentangle just like you would if you were meditating and free your mind of the worries and problems of the day, month, year, and lifetime. Remember that creating a Zentangle should feel ceremonial to you.

Step Six – Don't Stop

You'll know when it's time to put down the pen and stop, and when that time comes, you can stop. But don't stop before that moment and pick up the Zentangle later. It's about finishing something and staying focused long enough to accomplish it.

Once you're finished with your first Zentangle, frame it and keep it somewhere safe where you can enjoy it for a long time! You accomplished that and you should be proud.

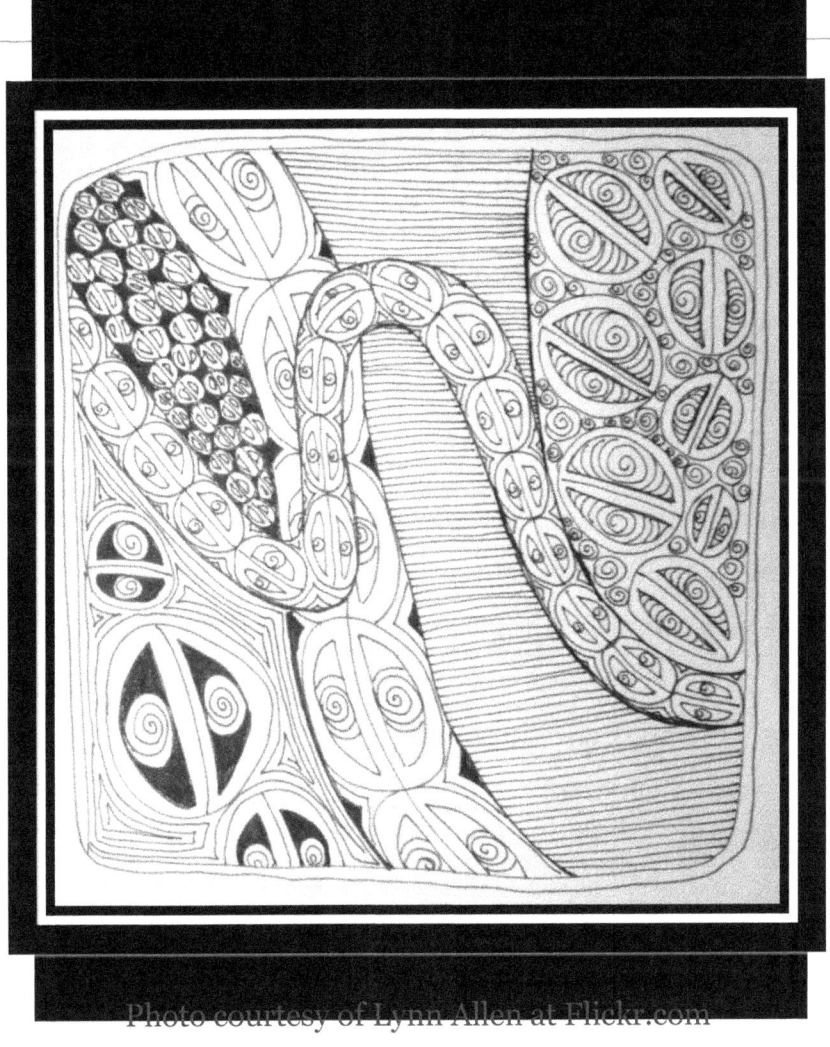

Now that you know how to create an original Zentangle let's take a look at some of the different patterns you can choose from to get you started. These patterns are going to make you look like an amazing Zentangle expert within minutes!

Chapter Four – Pattern Development

Before we get into the different patterns, let's talk more about how to develop those patterns. Each person will have unique patterns that they use and ones that they never thought they'd come up with as they're Zentangling. That's because there are no set patterns to Zentangle, unless you want to follow a format. Those formats can be found in the following chapter.

The most unique thing about Zentangle is that any line you draw is a pattern, no matter what you've put on the paper. Tangles do not have a preplanned guideline, dot, grid, or any erase lines. They're just a pen stroke on paper. Tangles are meant to be non-representational. They are intended to be this way so that you don't have to feel like you should be able to draw a hand or a dog well.

Tangle patterns are given names that don't hint at what they're supposed to look like so that there is no preconception of how a Zentangle should appear. That's why you should create a Zentangle on your own, without looking at patterns when you first begin. This allows you to really get a sense of the creativity and the focus that's needed to make one.

When recognizable objects or scenes are eliminated, thinking that's associated with those objects also goes. You're completely focused on the stroke of the abstract, pattern-making that has grown organically into a wonderful end result.

The process intentionally disrupts those thoughts that are not calming and replaces them with thoughts of where the next stroke of the pen is going to be.

So how do you define a tangle?

Well, a pattern is not always a Zentangle. These are the characteristics that will define a tangle for you:

- Tangles are two or three simple strokes of your pen.
- Tangles are easy enough to draw without using a preprinted grid. You also should not be using a pencil underneath to sketch out the design before you draw. Inked dots and grids can be part of the tangle, though.
- A tangle is not going to use stencils, rulers, or another type of mechanical aid.
- A tangle is a non-objective, abstract art form.
- Tangles do not have directions, meaning it can be positioned any way for it to be viewed.
- Tangles are an overall pattern rather than a single motif.
- Tangles are unique and elegant.

So now that you know how to develop a pattern of your own let's look at some premade ones to give you an idea of what you can start with.

Chapter Five – The Simplicity of Patterns and Styles

There are many different forms of patterns and styles for Zentangles, but remember that a pattern should only be a few pen strokes at most. Let's take a look at some of the most popular patterns and styles out there.

Cadent

This is a fun tangle that's pretty easy to do. First, you draw some squares, as shown.

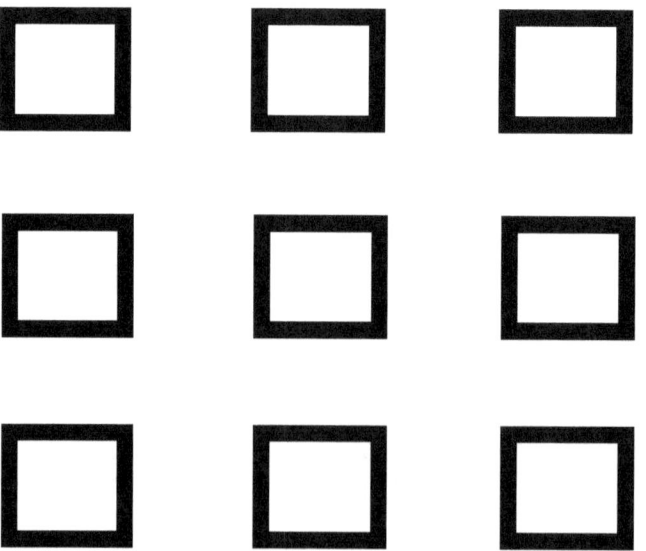

Photo courtesy of Author

Next, attach those squares together starting at the top left corner square. Draw a line from the bottom right corner of that square to the top left corner of the square beneath it. Like so:

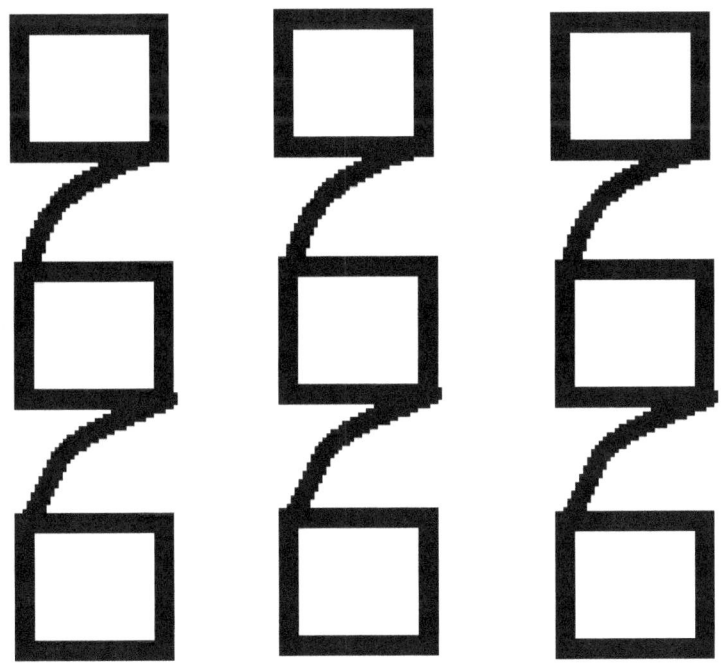

Photo courtesy of Author

Once you have all the boxes connected vertically, it's time to connect them horizontally by connection the top right of the box you began with to the bottom left of the box directly to the right of it, like so:

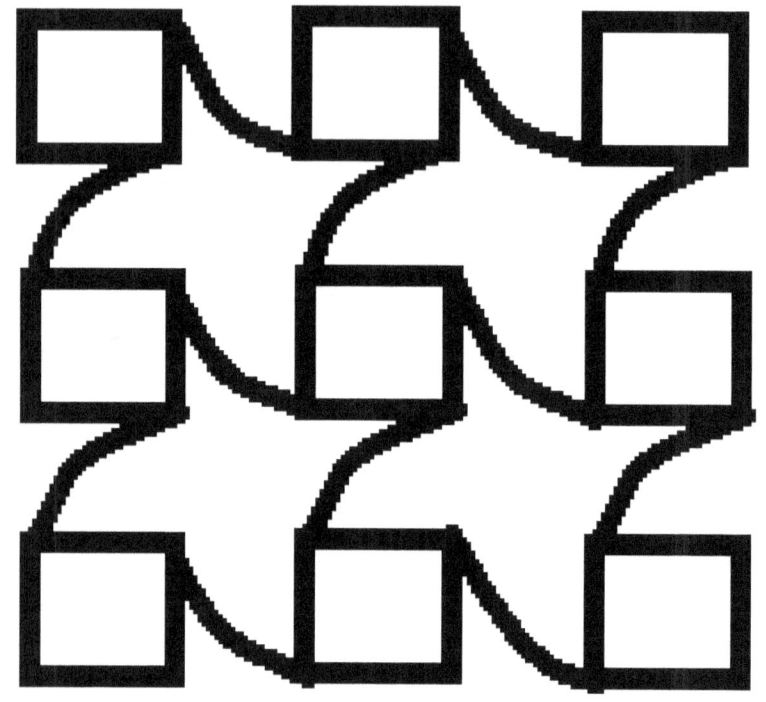

Photo courtesy of Author

Keep in mind that in no way does it have to be perfect, and you can use as many boxes and lines as you'd like to connect them. But this is just a start with the Cadent Pattern.

Jonqal

This is a bold tangle that is actually very three-dimensional when it's shaded in.

First, draw four lines within your border as such:

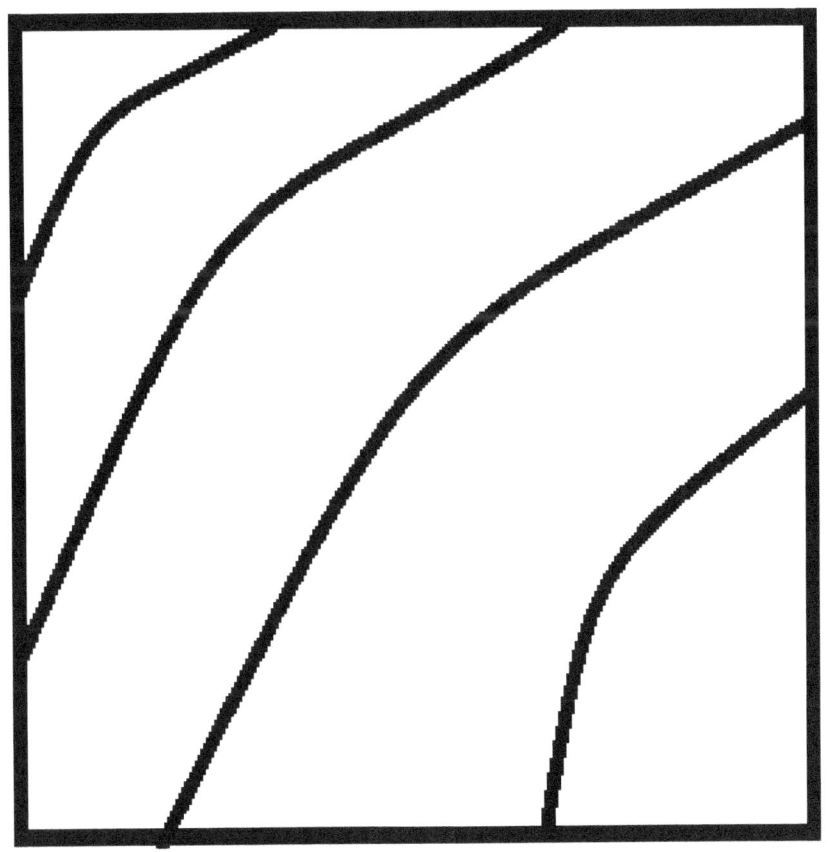

Photo courtesy of Author

Next, draw steps going down from those lines, like this:

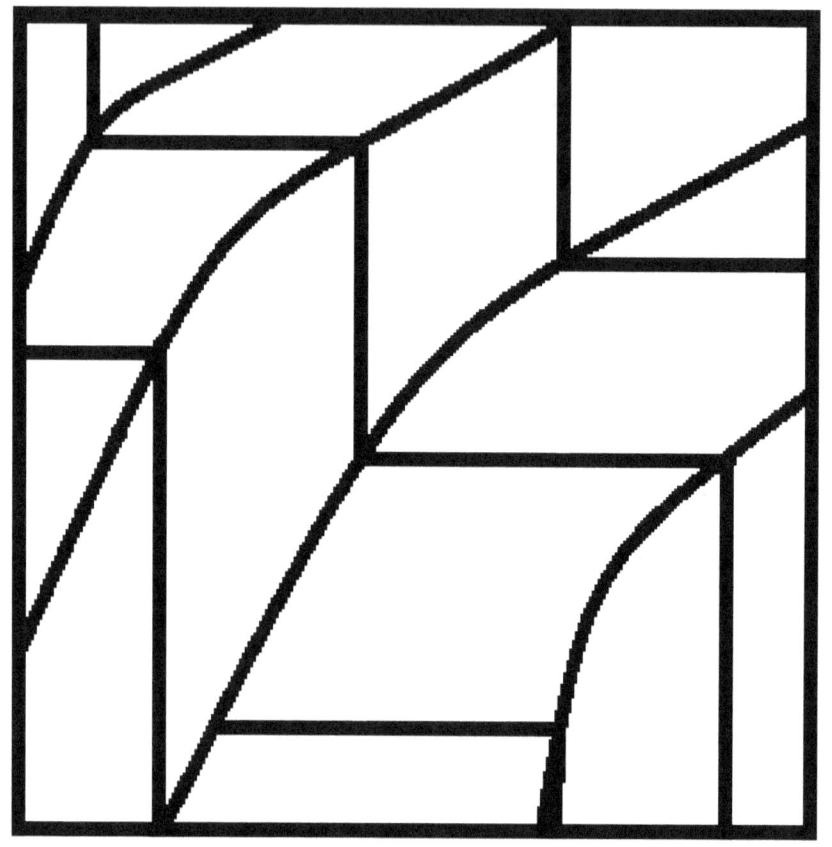

Photo courtesy of Author

By the time you're finished, it almost looks like a set of stairs going up from bottom right to top left. You then shade in every other block like so:

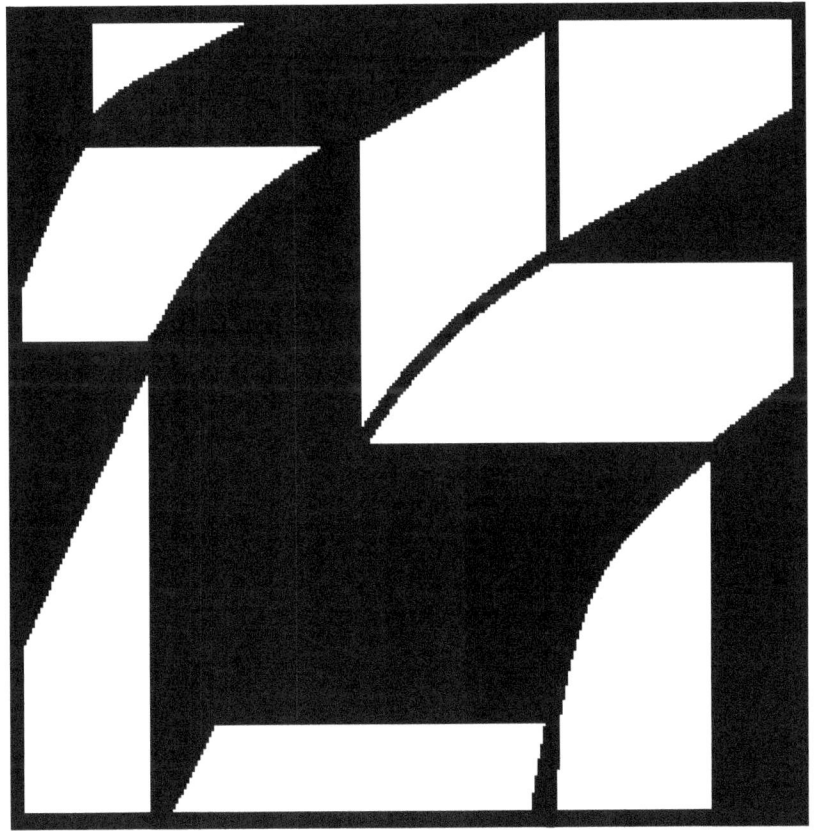

Photo courtesy of Author

Depending on where you shade, it'll look different from someone else's, and it also depends on where you draw the stair lines.

Paradox

Paradox seems like a very complex tangle when you first look at it but don't be intimidated by it! It's actually pretty easy to draw. Here are the instructions.

First, draw a triangle sort of like this in your square:

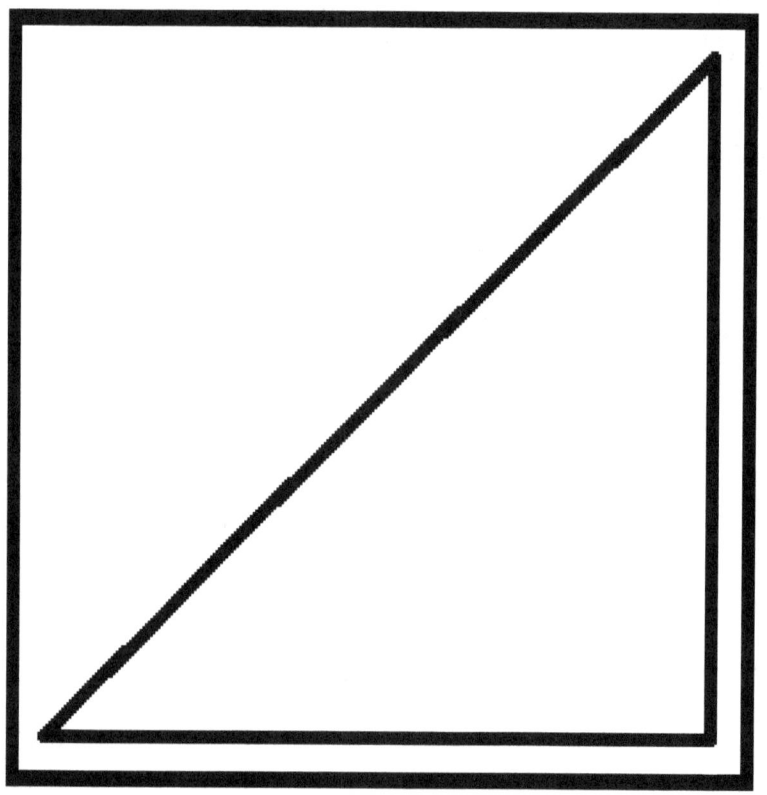

Photo courtesy of Author

Then you draw the next set of lines like this:

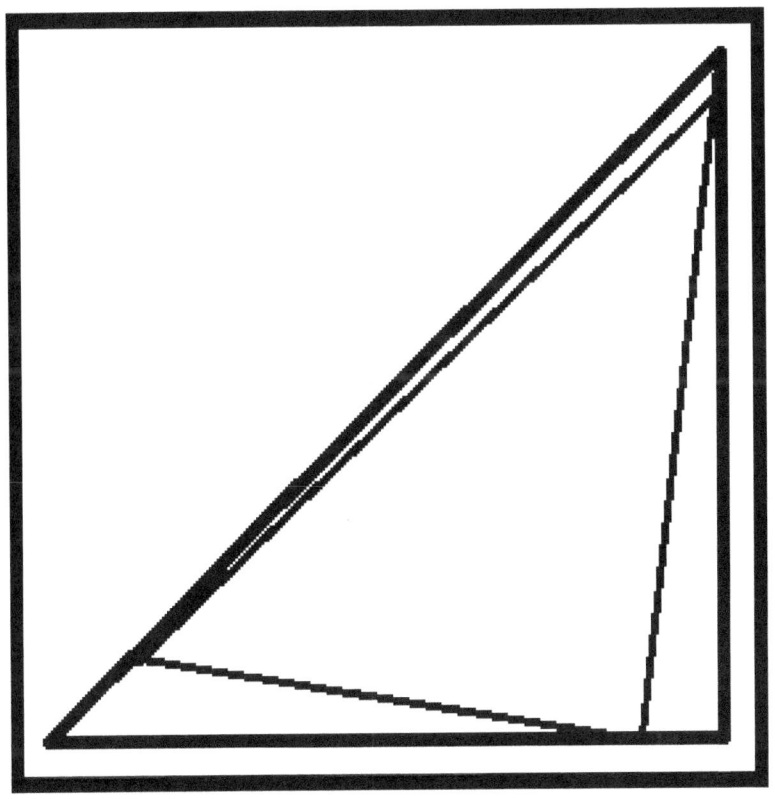

Photo courtesy of Author

And keep going in that same pattern until you end up with something that looks similar to this:

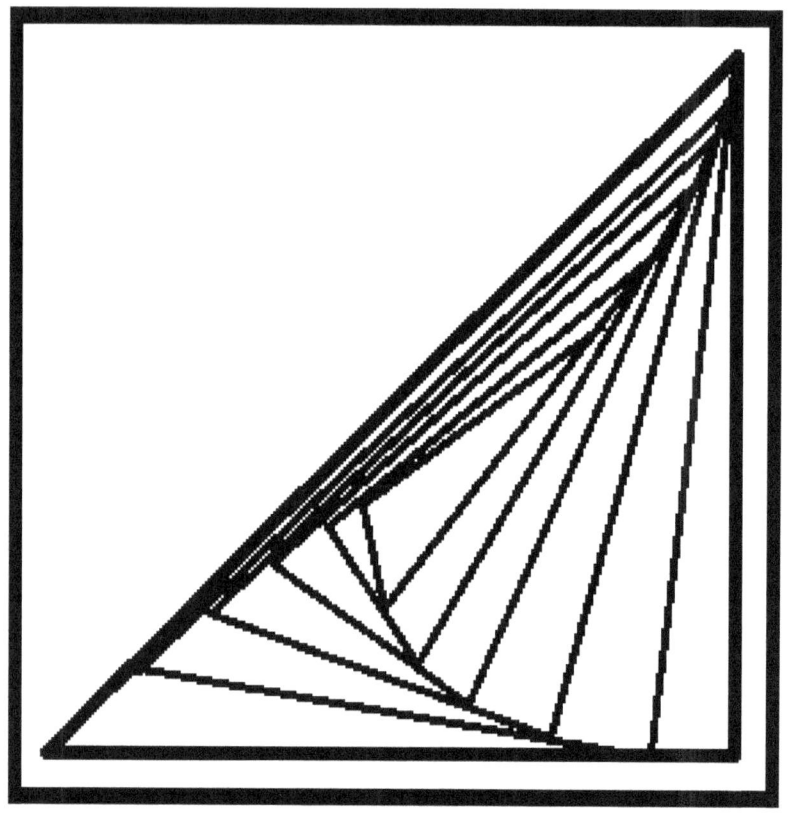

Photo courtesy of Author

As you can see, it looks sort of complex, but it's really not. And it doesn't have to be perfect. Once you add in different patterns to the empty space, it'll blend in nicely.

Opus

Opus is another tangle that looks rather difficult, but it's not. It can take you many directions once you're done with the main part of the tangle. Draw the first lines as such:

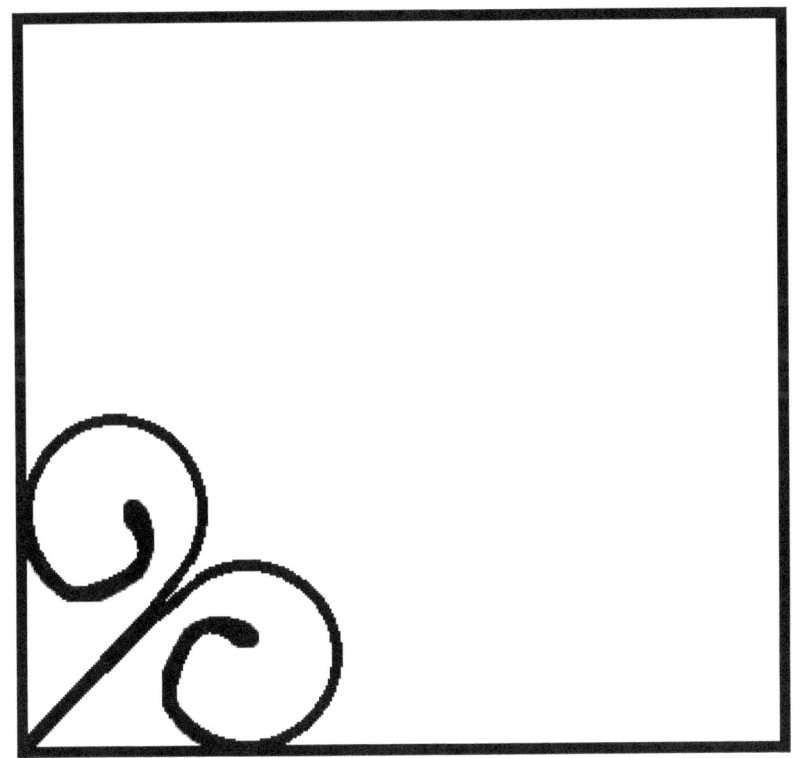

Photo courtesy of Author

Once you're done with those two, follow the pattern up the square like this:

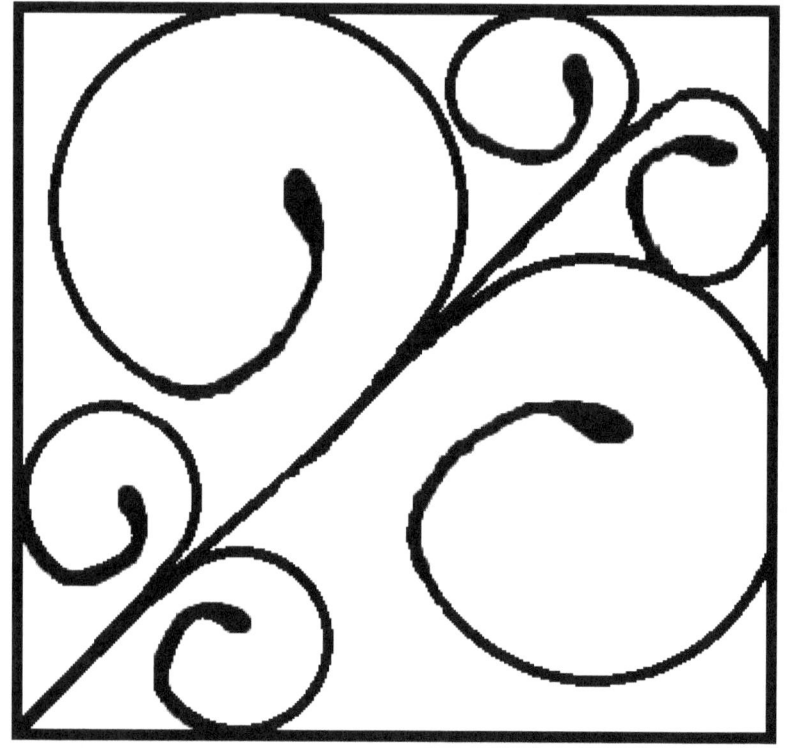

Photo courtesy of Author

When you're finished with adding in the half circles, you can then add in bubbles or even trace along the outside with an aura pattern. We'll get into the aura in a bit.

XYP

This pattern is pronounced 'zip' and was found on some old bills. It looks hard, but it's just like the others. It's very simple! So let's check it out.

First, you'll need to draw a string as such:

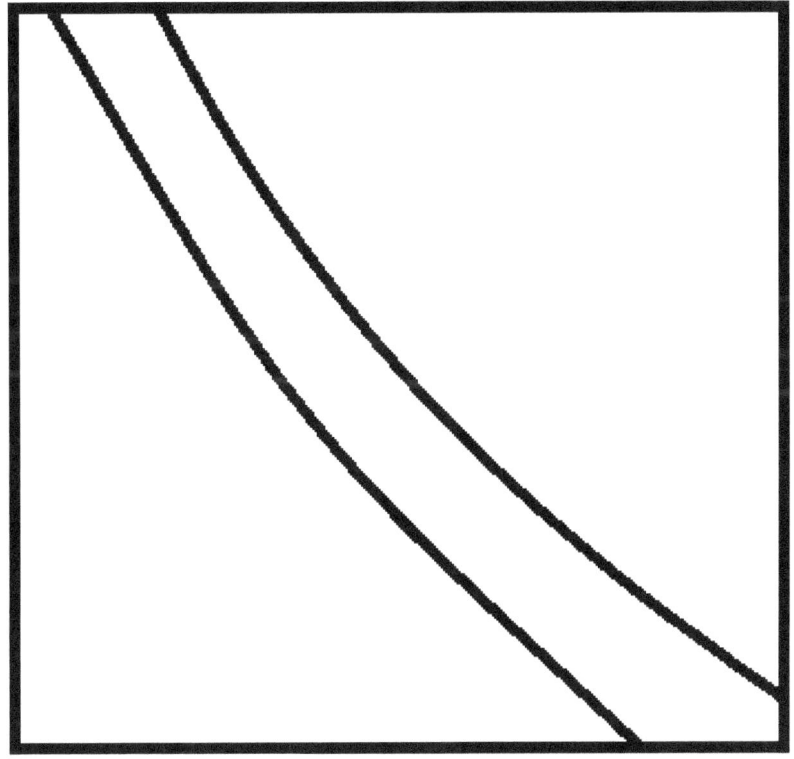

Photo courtesy of Author

Remember strings are traditionally drawn in pencil so you won't see them. Then you'll need to draw some x's inside of those lines.

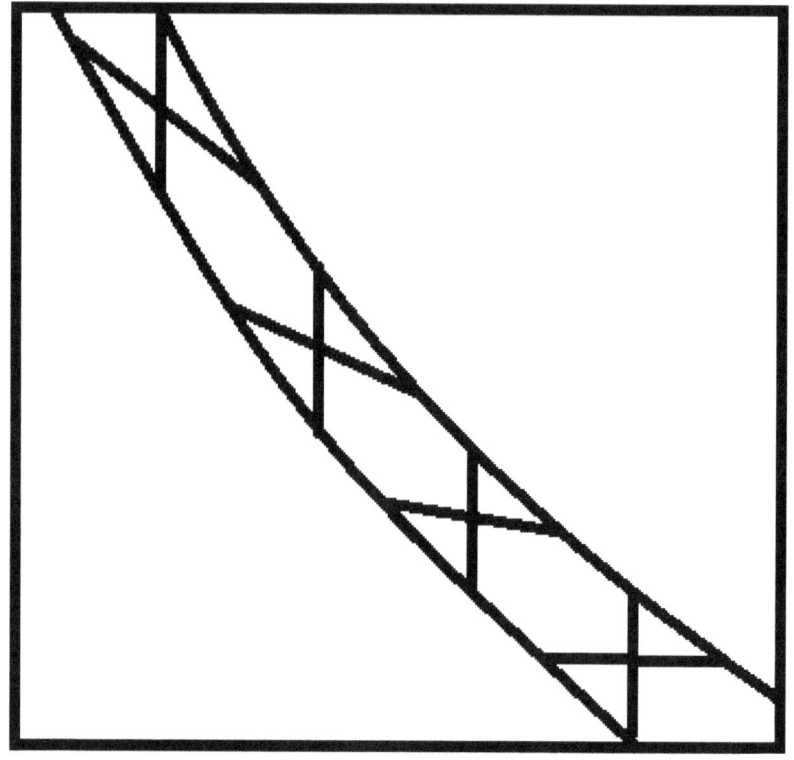

Photo courtesy of Author

Next, you'll need to draw some lines to attach those x's like this:

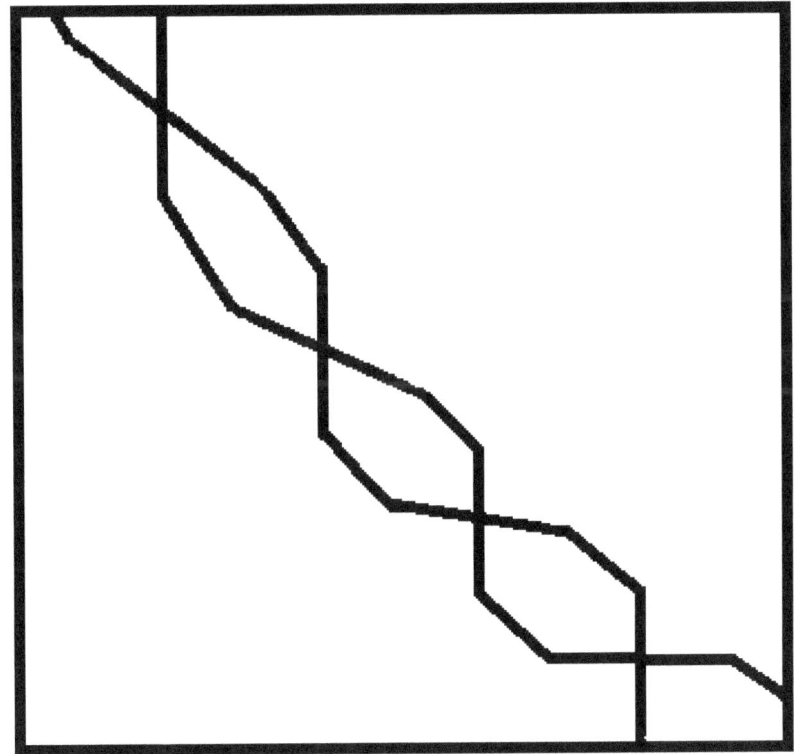

Photo courtesy of Author

As you can see, the connecting lines follow the string line, but the rest of it is gone. Now you'll need to draw squares on top of the x's like this:

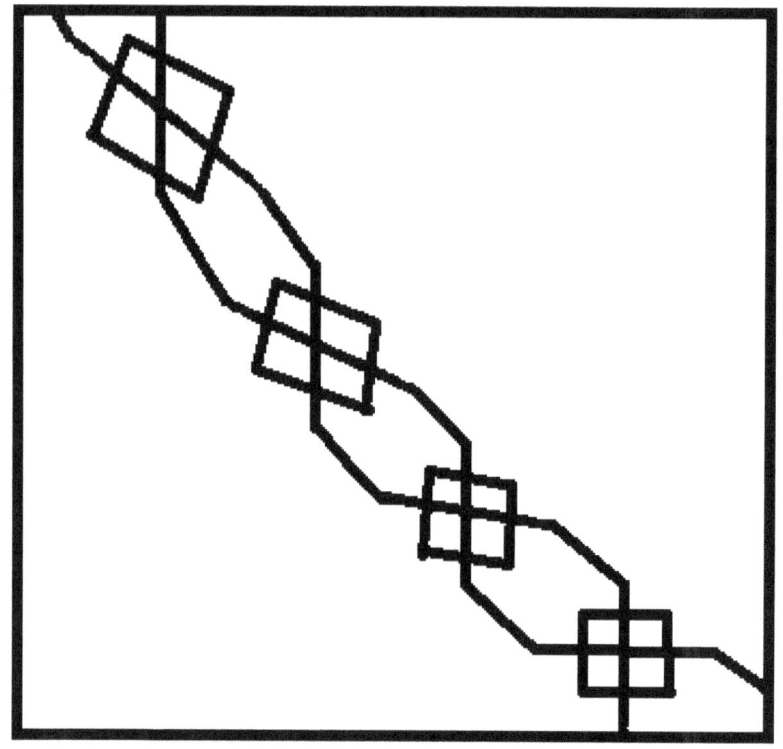

Photo courtesy of Author

Now that you have the boxes, draw some connection lines between the box points inside pattern like this:

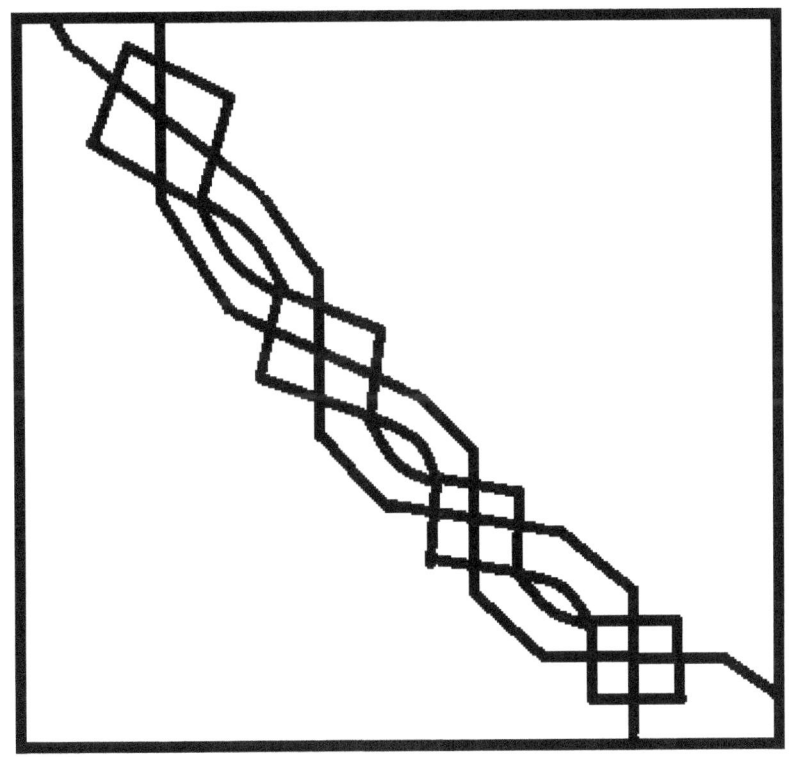

Photo courtesy of Author

Now that you have the ovals drawn on the inside, you'll be doing a little shading.

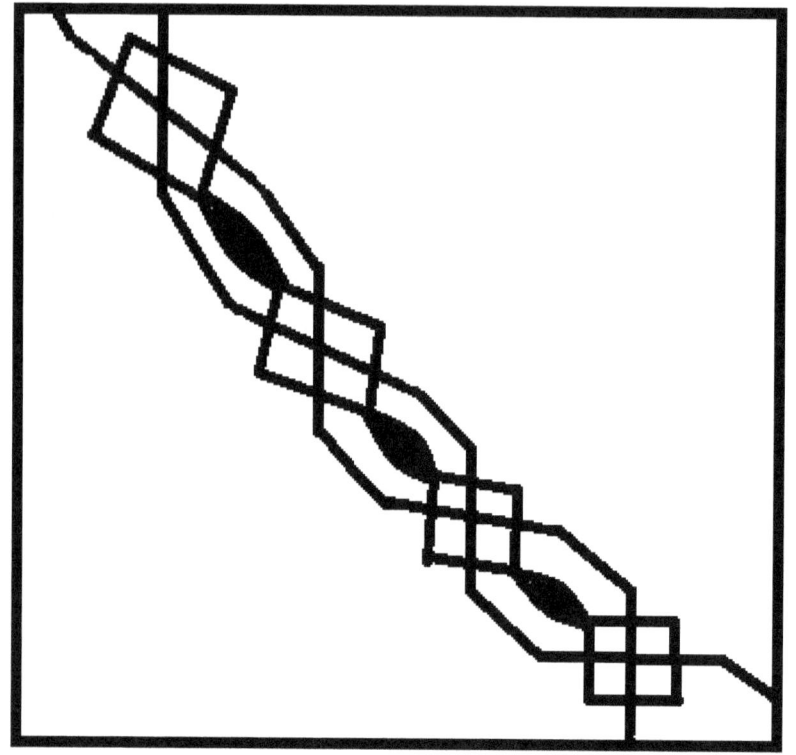

Photo courtesy of Author

Some choose to add in an aura on the outside of the pattern, but you'll be shown how to do that in a later chapter.

Cubine

The cubine is a very easy pattern to accomplish. It's full of contrast and is able to be done with straight or curved lines. Practice the straight first before you try the curved to get a feel for the pattern.

Start with your square and four lines like this:

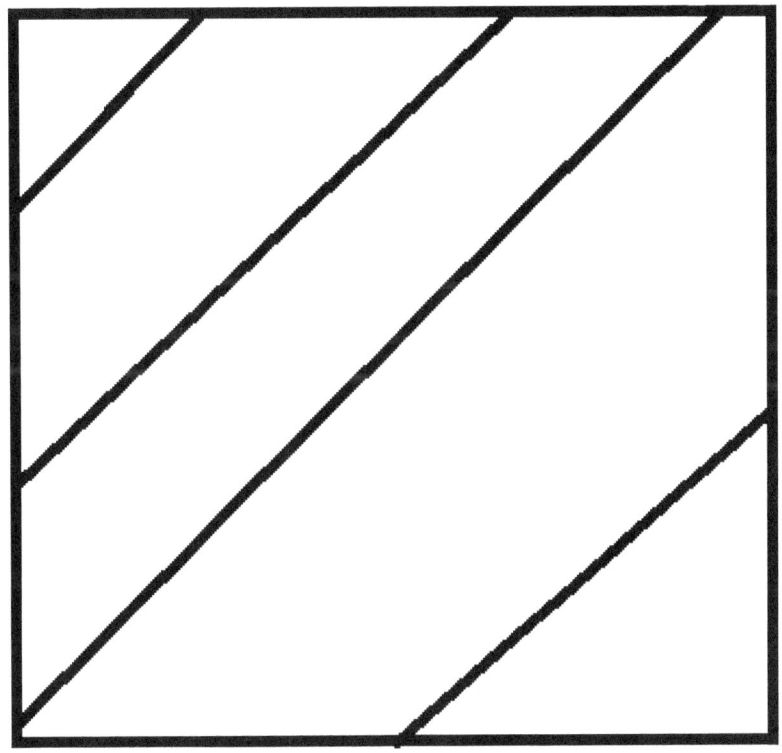

Photo courtesy of Author

Then add in some lines facing the opposite direction like this:

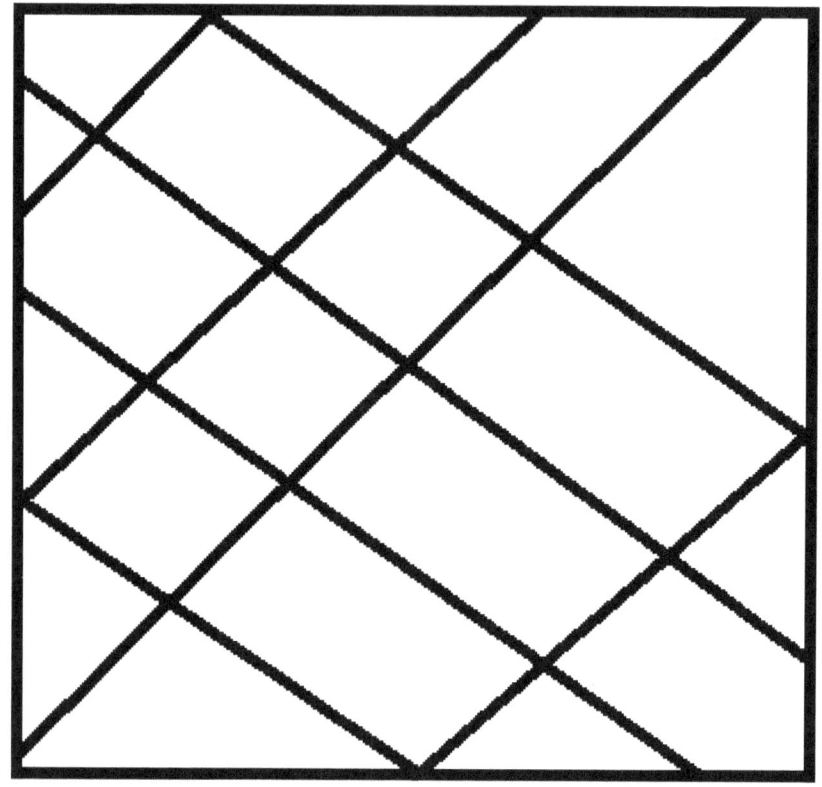

Photo courtesy of Author

Remember that no line is ever perfect in Zentangle, and that's what makes it art! Now add in some squares to those diamonds you have like this:

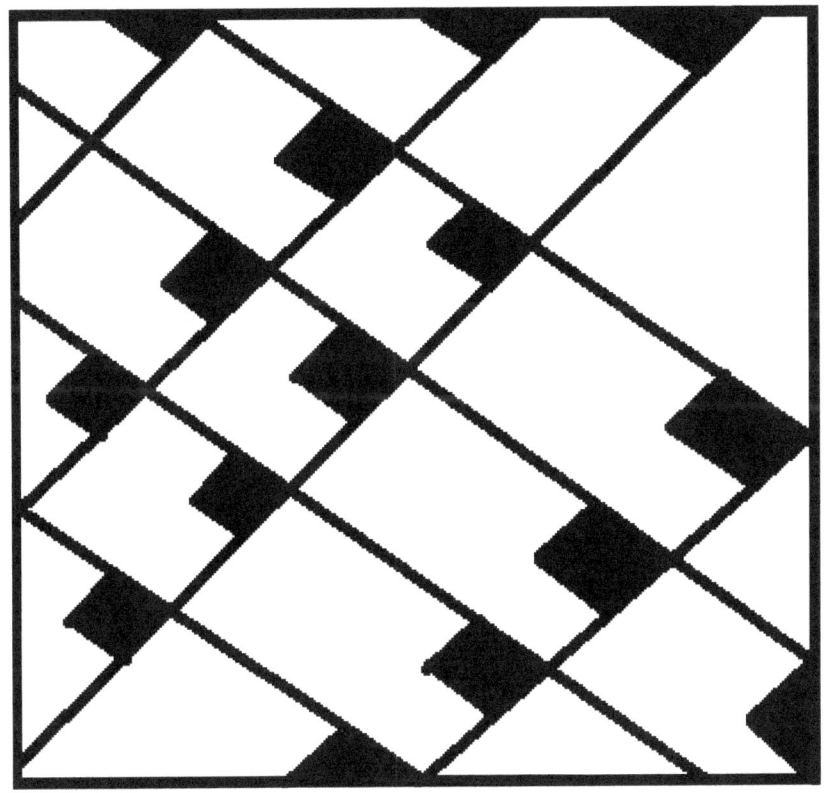

Photo courtesy of Author

Once you're done shading those in, you can now add some lines like this:

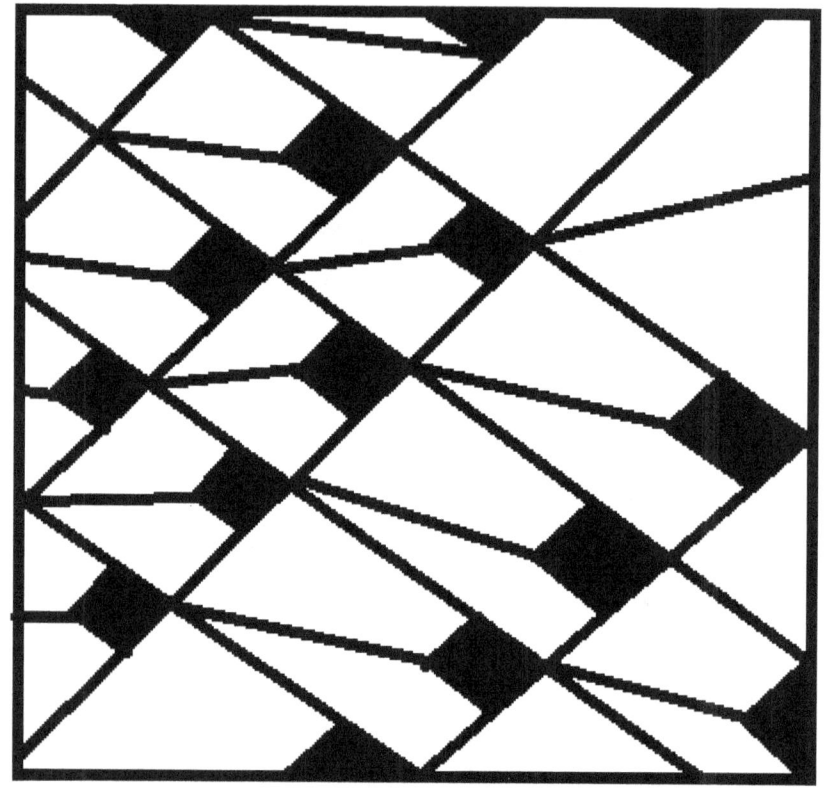

Photo courtesy of Author

Some will then choose to shade in the top half of the space they created, such as this:

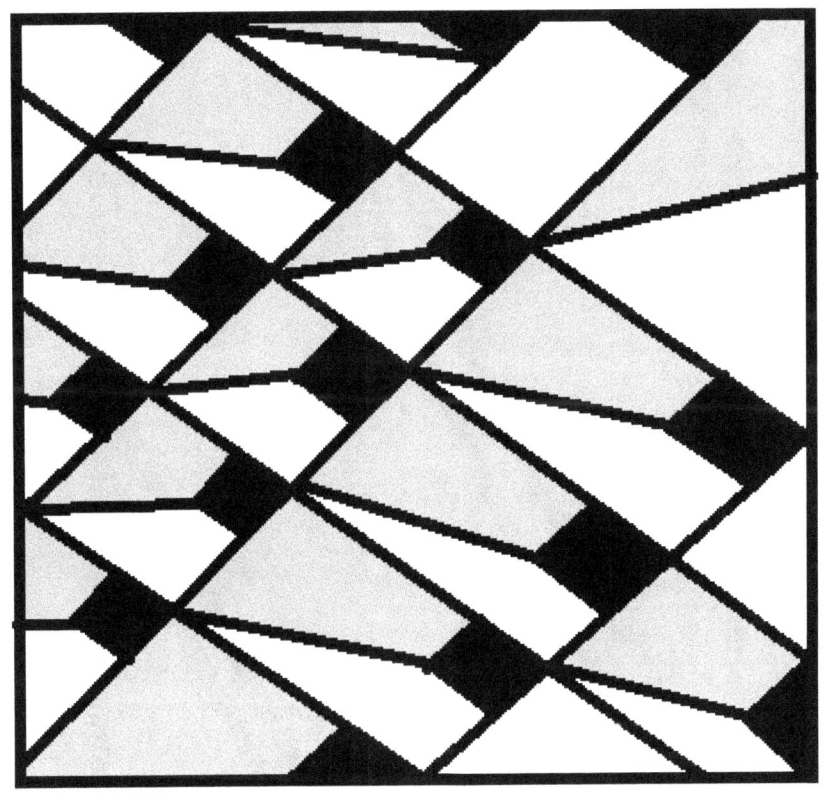

Photo courtesy of Author

You can choose to leave it blank, though if you prefer the other look.

Hibred

The hibred is many steps, but the end result is very neat.

First, you draw four lines like this:

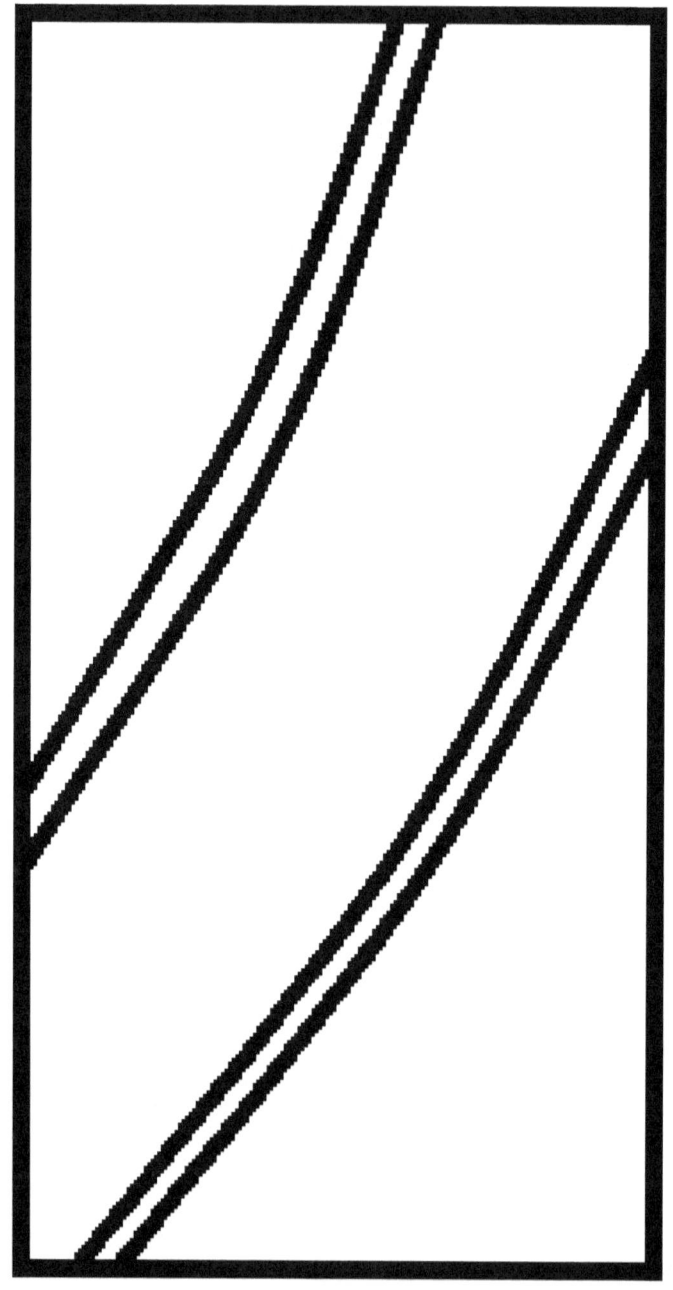

Photo courtesy of Author

Next, you'll need to add some triangles like this:

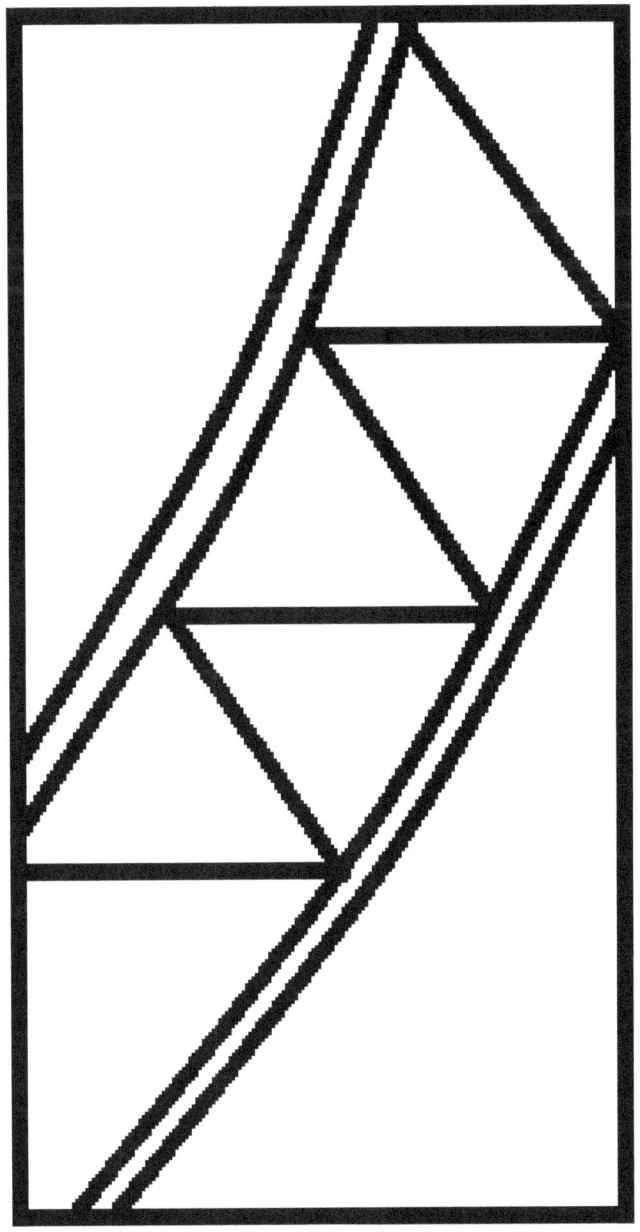

Photo courtesy of Author

Now add some connection like this:

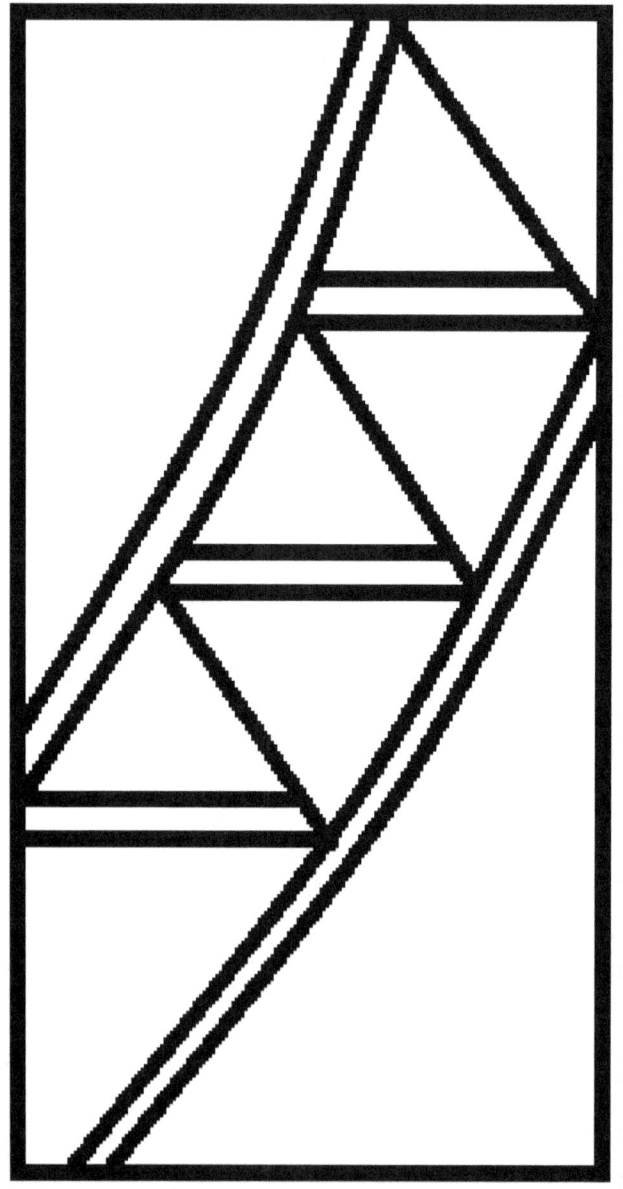

Photo courtesy of Author

And some lines like this:

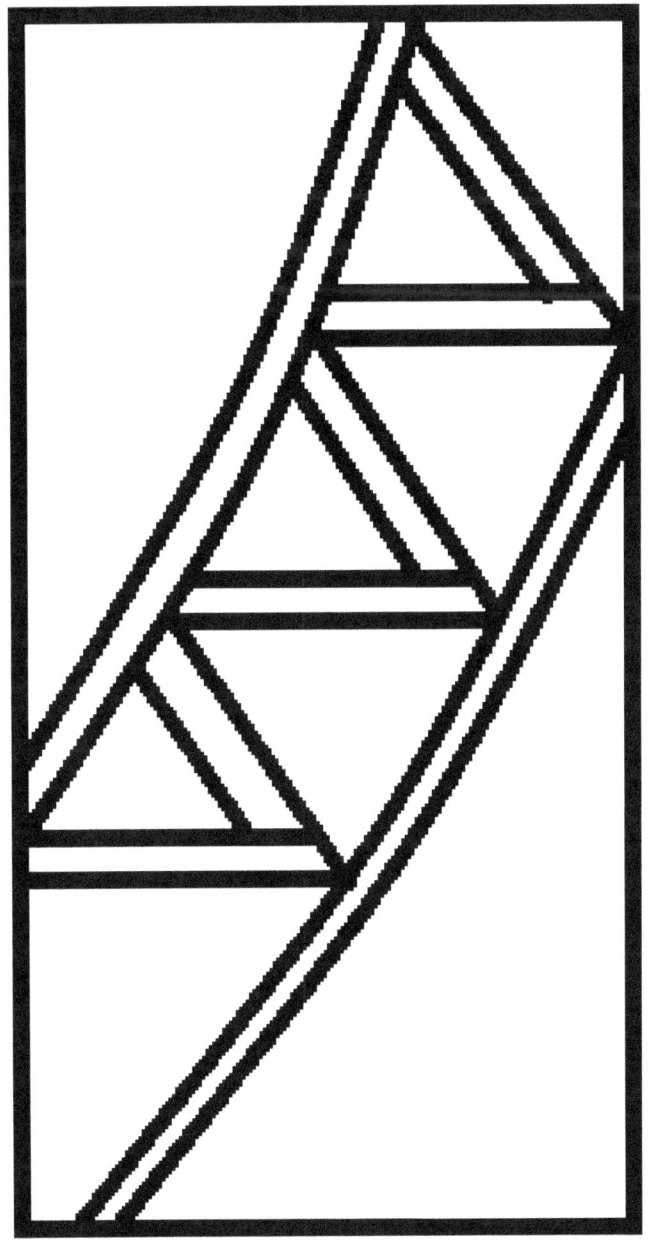

Photo courtesy of Author

And continue to follow that pattern until you have this result:

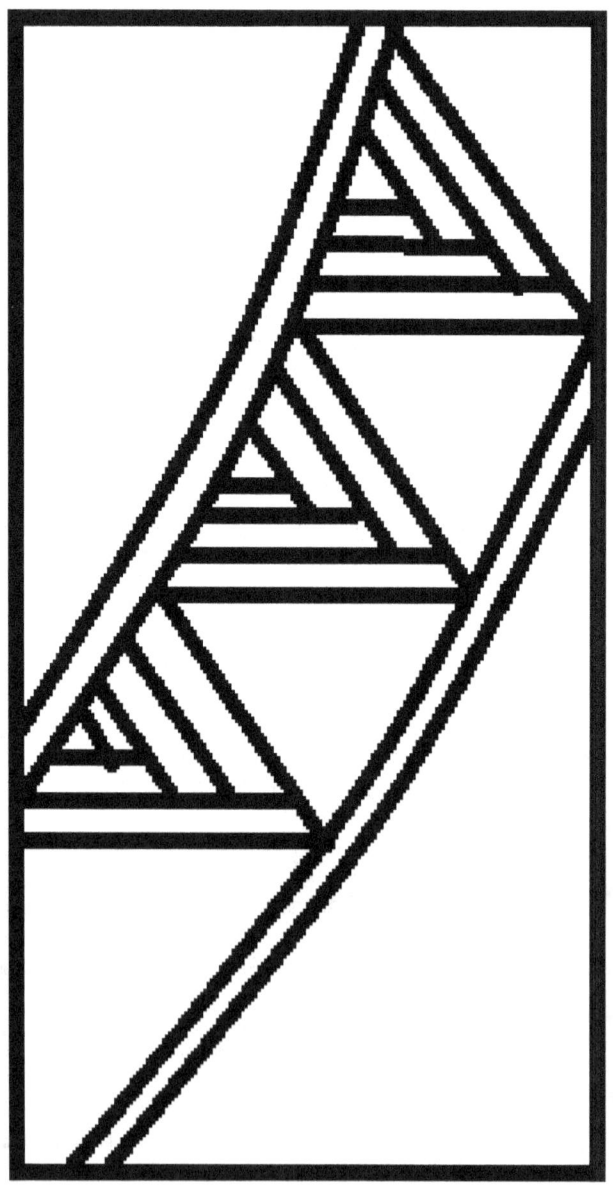

Photo courtesy of Author

Then follow the pattern on the other side like so:

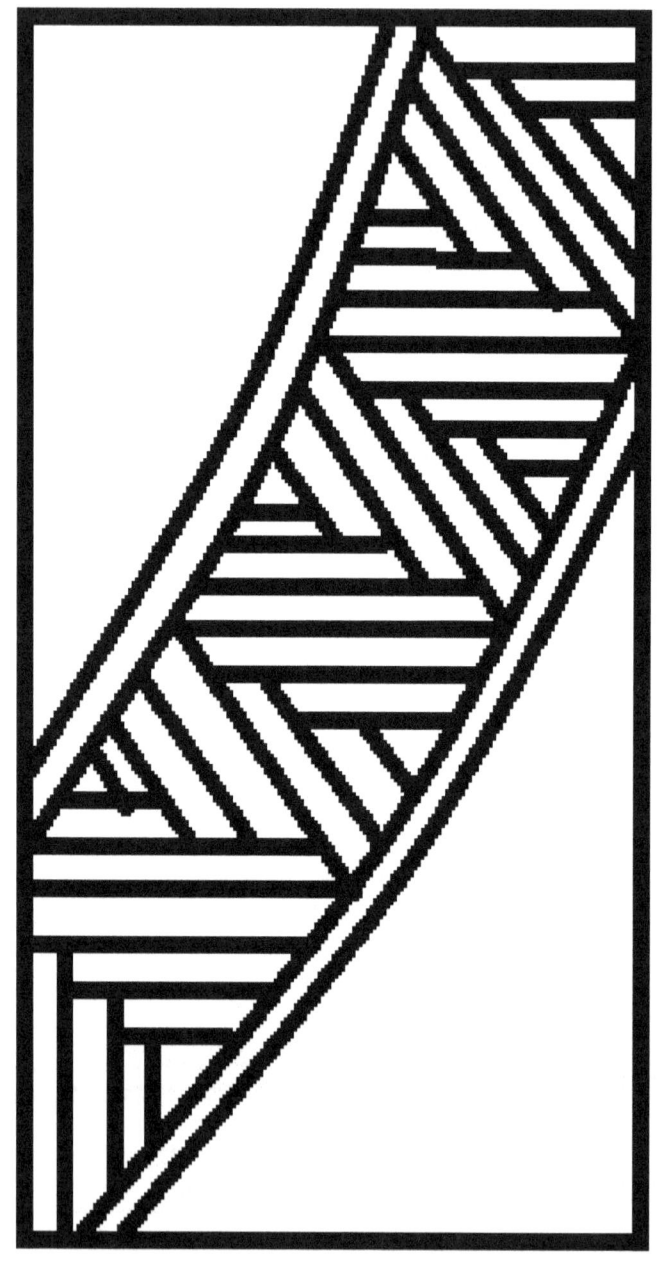

Photo courtesy of Author

And when you're finished, you have this piece of art that looks really complex, but it's not! You can choose to shade in part of the design or shade the empty spaces to give it a more three-dimensional look, or just leave it as it is.

Sez

This is a pretty awesome tangle that was inspired by an aboriginal painting.

First, you put some dots on random parts of the tile like this:

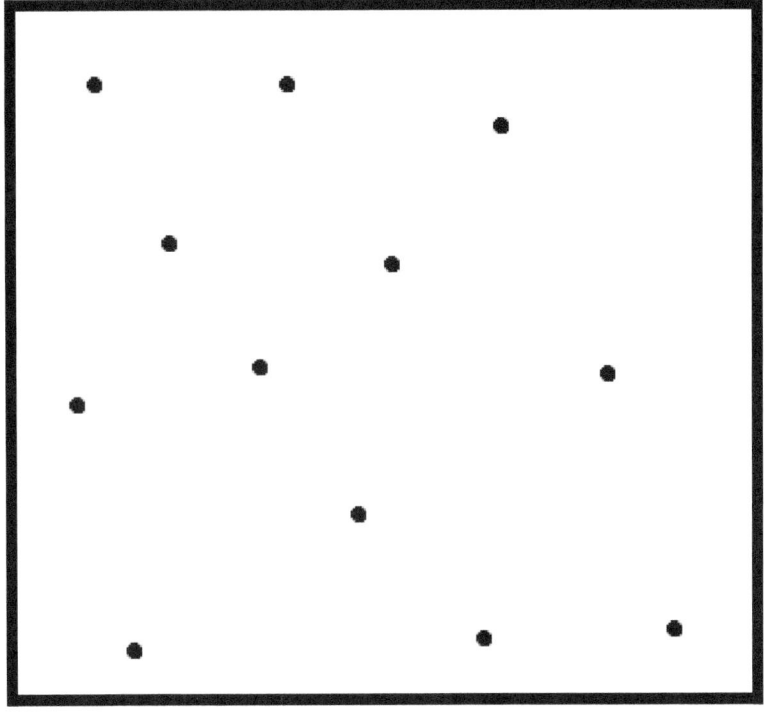

Photo courtesy of Author

Then you draw some circles around those dots.

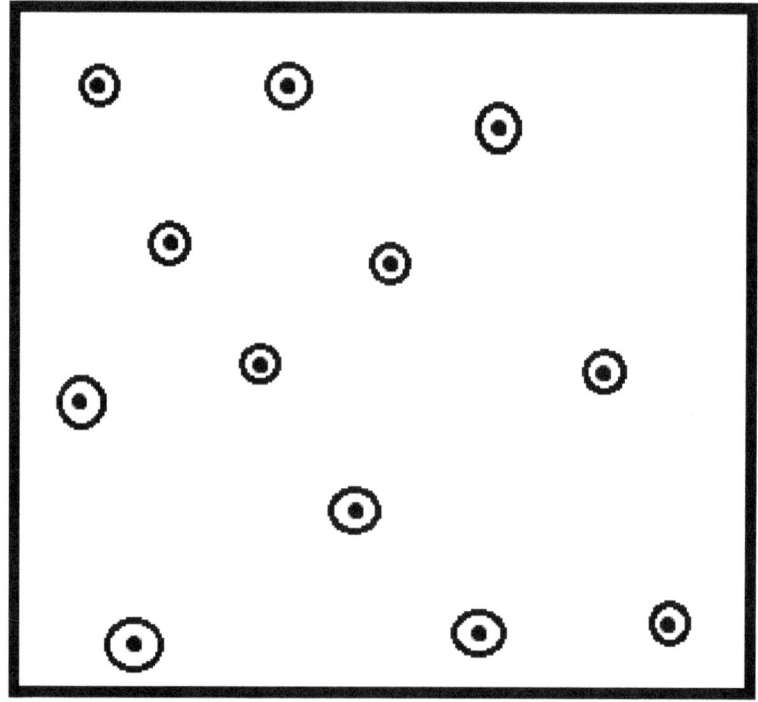

Photo courtesy of Author

And then keep drawing them until they begin to connect, like
this:

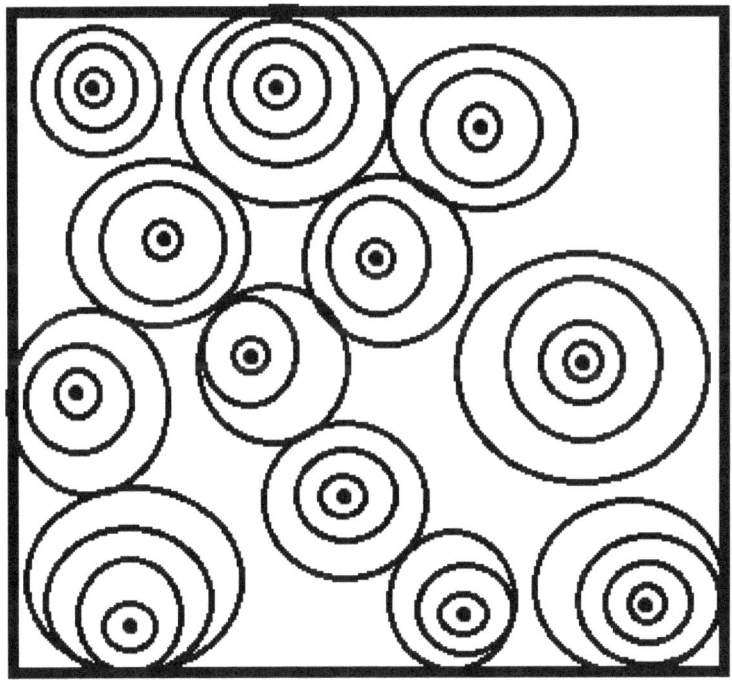

Photo courtesy of Author

Once they've connected, you can then add in some aura, like
this:

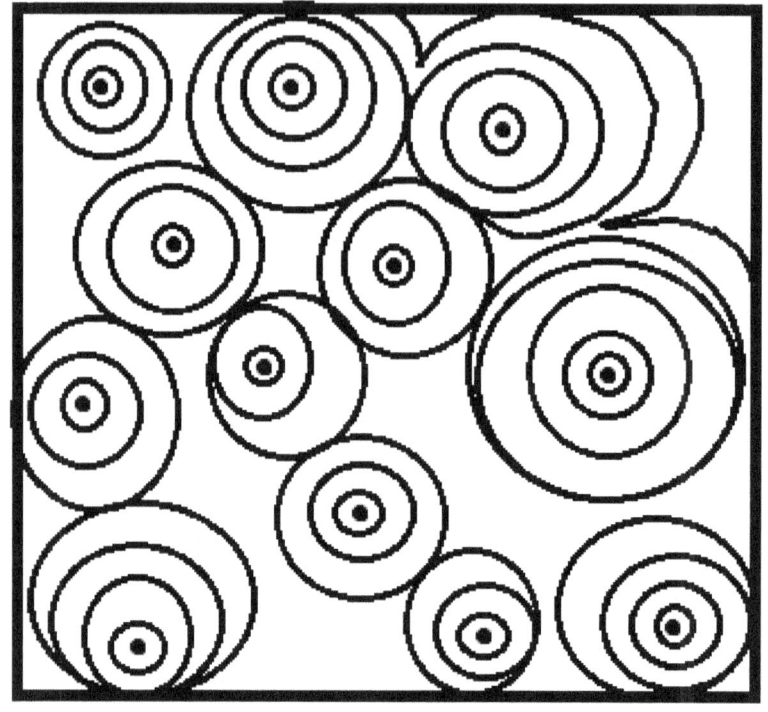

Photo courtesy of Author

And continue until you have no more white space left.

Hurry

This is a very nice looking tangle that is very, very simple to complete.

Draw three lines on your tile like this:

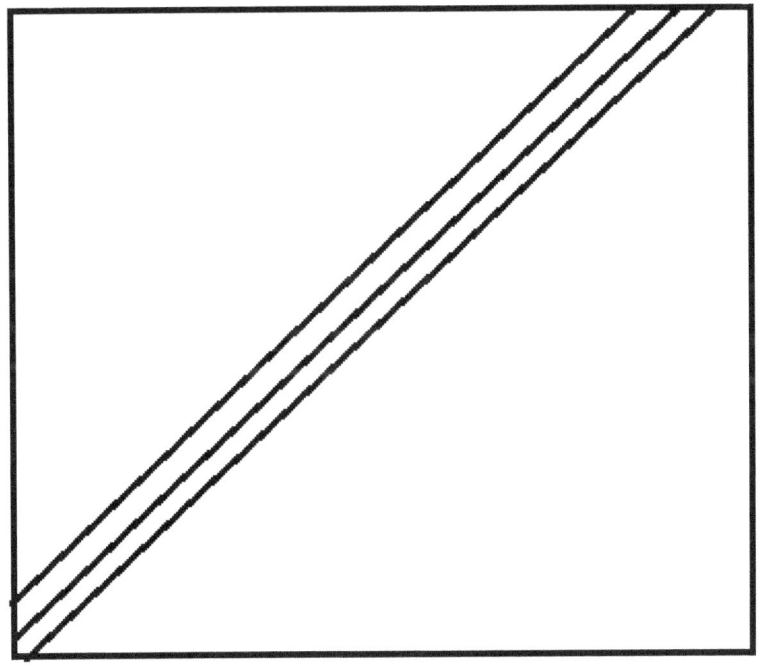

Photo courtesy of Author

Now draw three more corresponding lines like this:

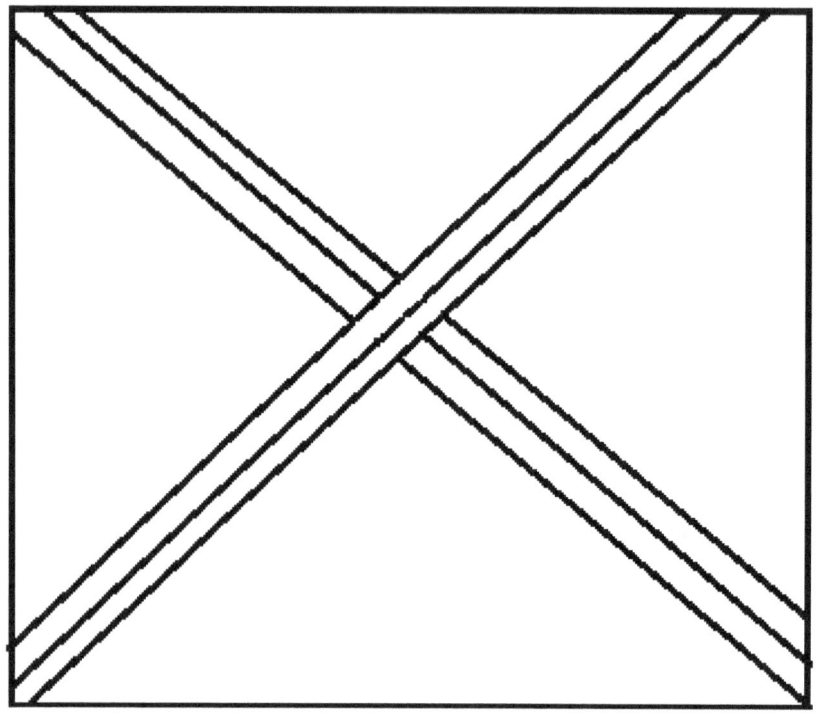

Photo courtesy of Author

Now draw three vertical lines like this:

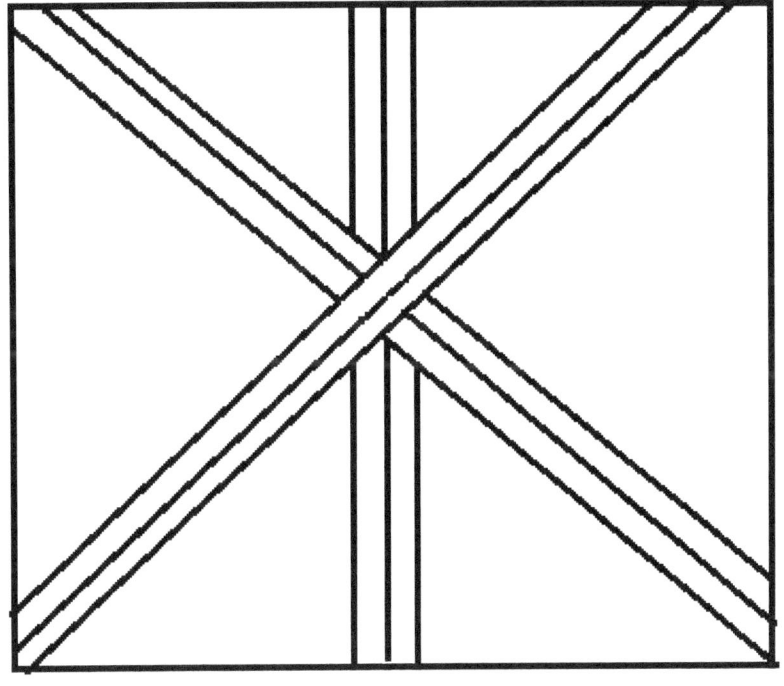

Photo courtesy of Author

And three more horizontal lines like this:

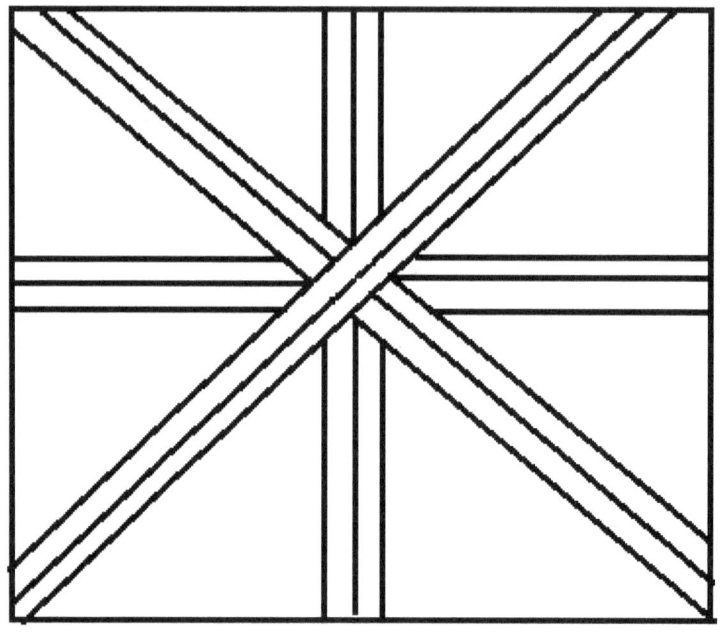

Photo courtesy of Author

And now that you have the pattern down continue to follow it through.

Munchin

This one is really great shaded, so be sure to try doing that!

First, you want to draw a series of dots on the tile like this:

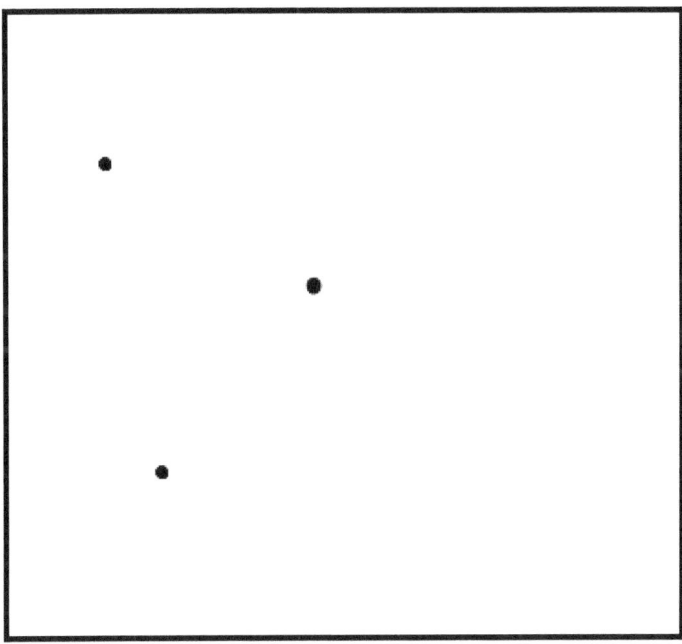

Photo courtesy of Author

You can draw more dots to get a more in-depth Zentangle, but I'm only using three for demonstrative purposes. When you have your dots, you will then connect them together with lines, like this.

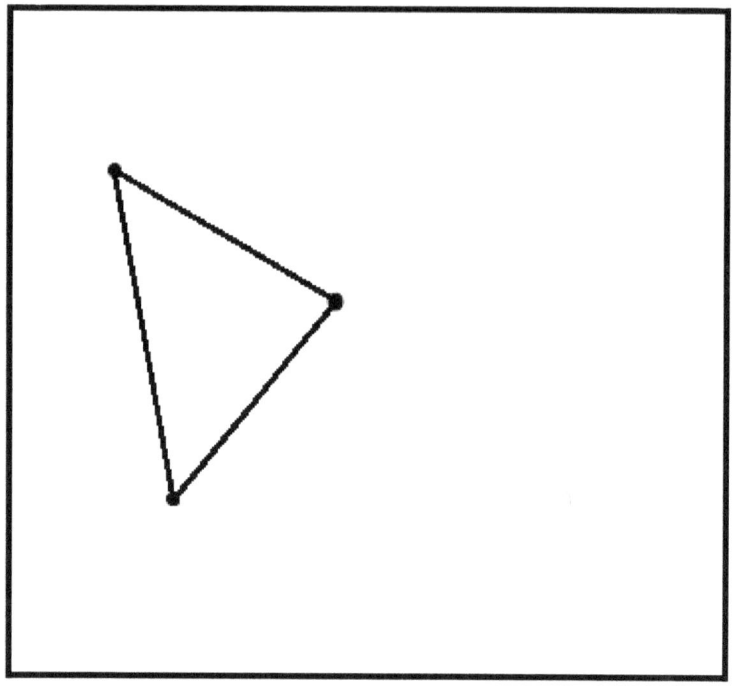

Photo courtesy of Author

Now that you've created an enclosed area fill in that area with some parallel lines, like this.

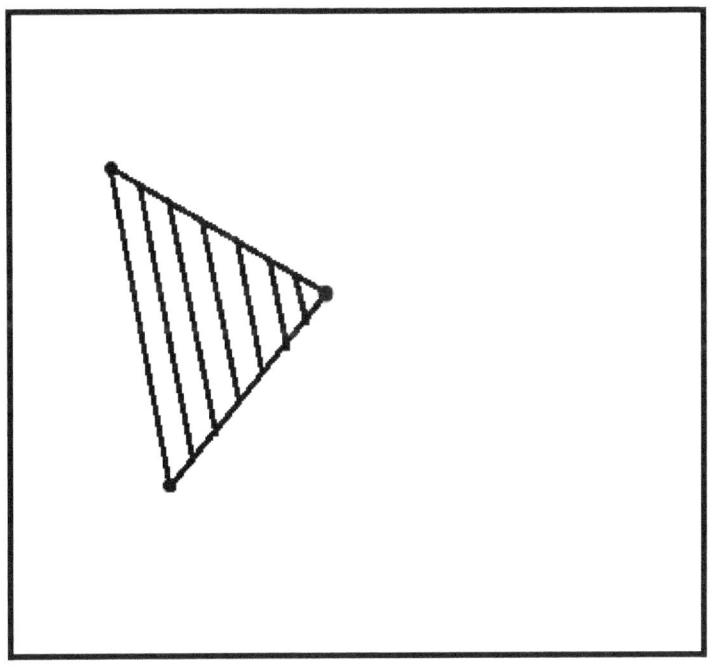

Photo courtesy of Author

Once you're done with all of the lines and the dots have been connected, the end result should look a lot like this:

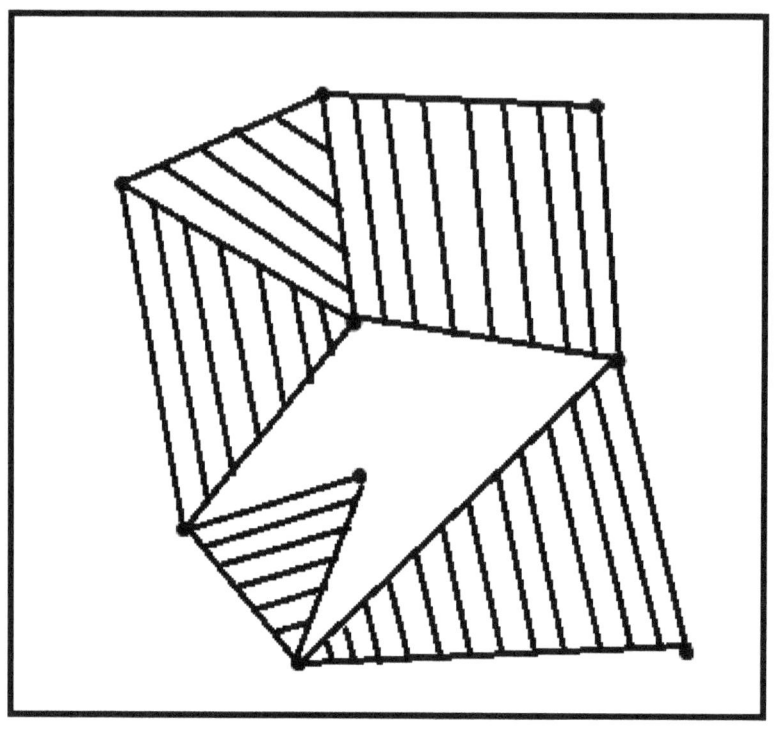

Photo courtesy of Author

Meer

Meer is a great tangle to mix in with other tangles in order to make it really pop, and it's an excellent border if you're doing something decorative.

First, start with four lines like you did with Hibred. Like this:

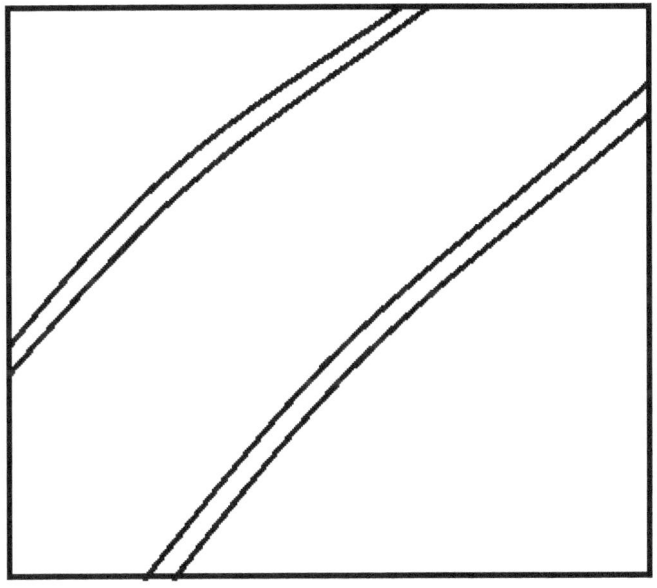

Photo courtesy of Author

Then insert a string in between like this:

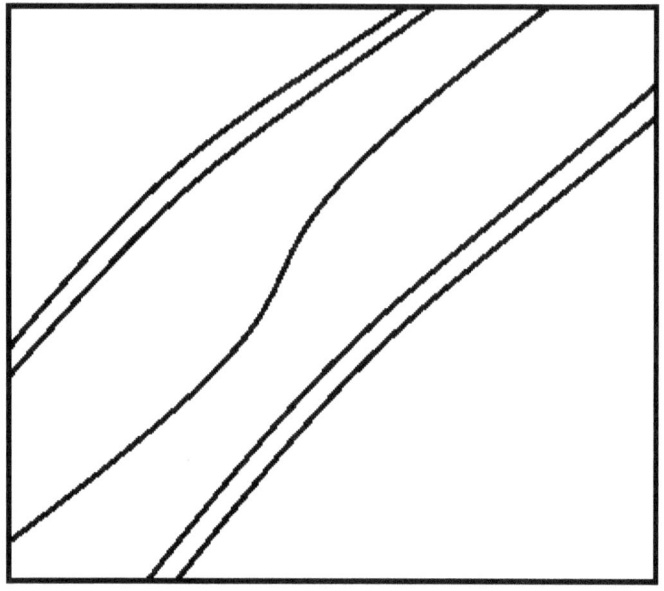

Photo courtesy of Author

Once you have the string, start to add some bubbles on the outside of the four lines like this:

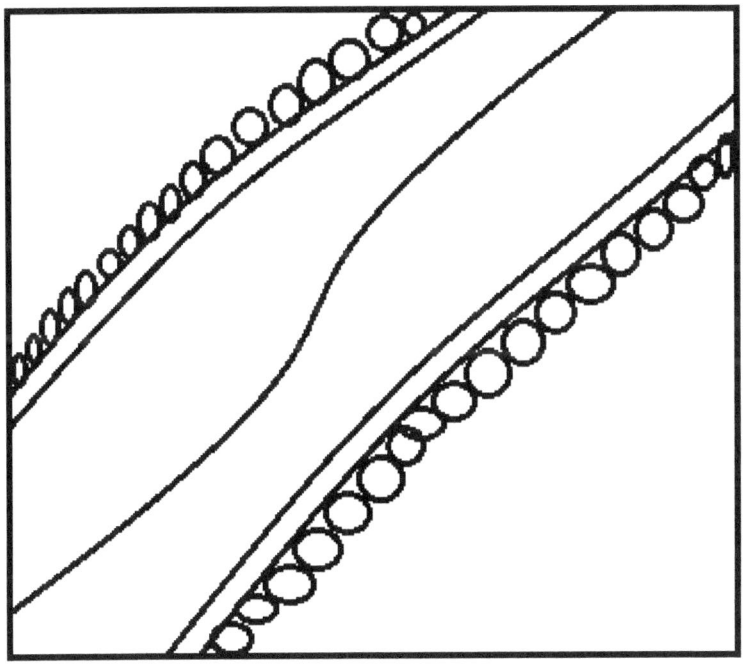

Photo courtesy of Author

Next, add some vertical lines to the bottom of the inside half of the pattern, like this:

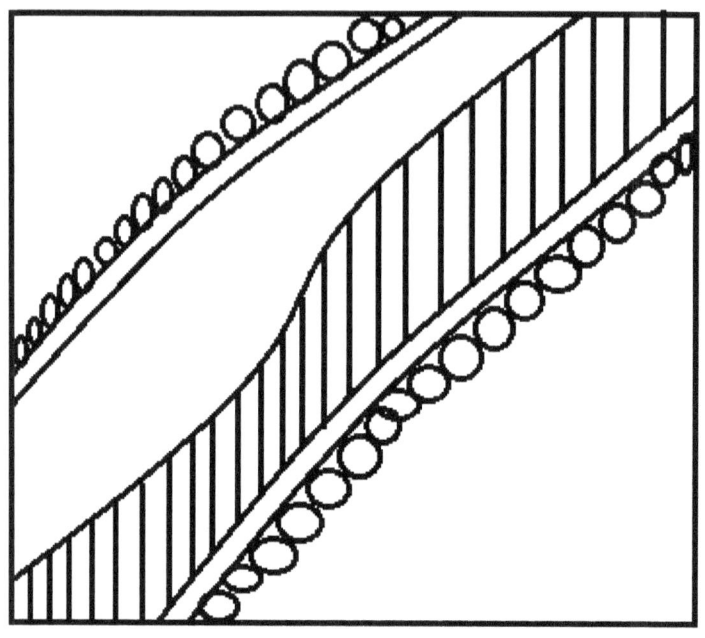

Photo courtesy of Author

Now add some corresponding lines to those lines on the other side that are horizontal.

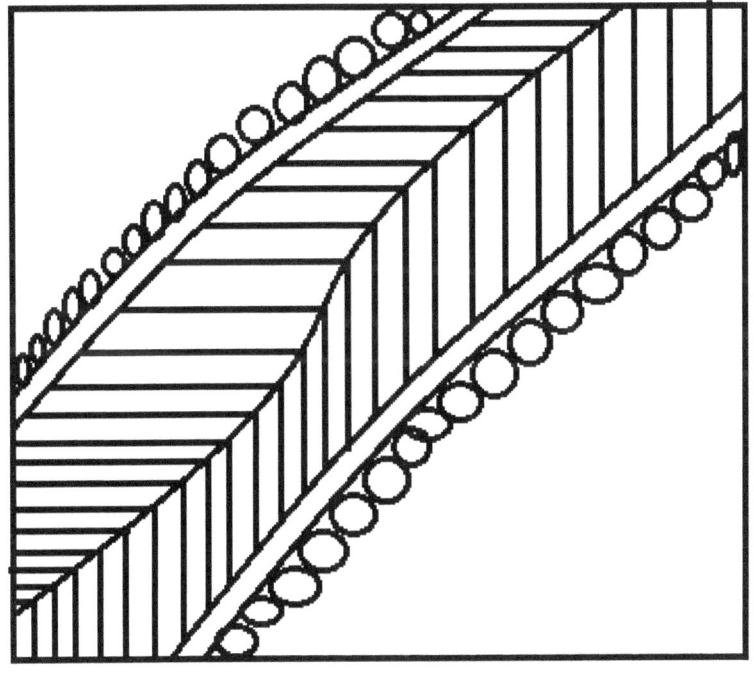

Photo courtesy of Author

Now that you have those, shade in some of the spaces with a pencil or a pen to make it look more three dimensional.

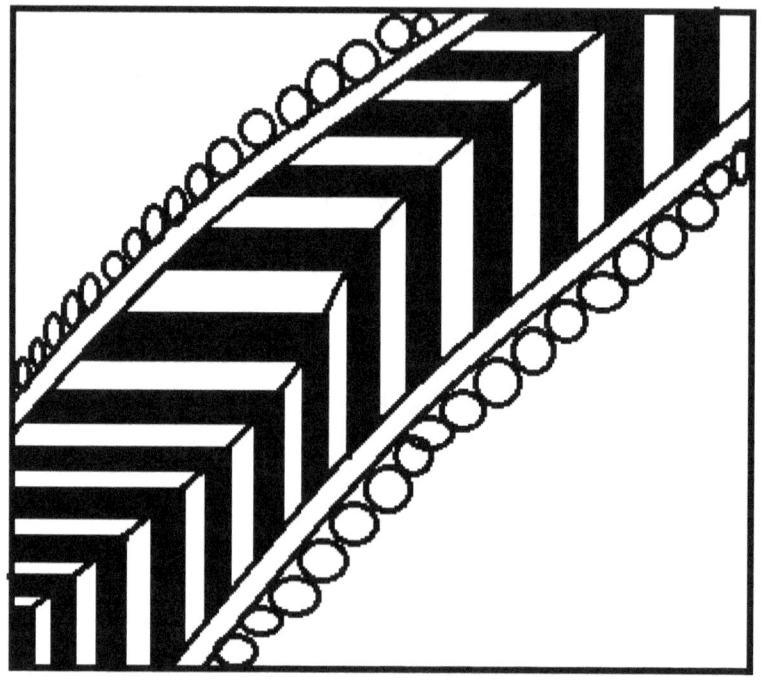

Photo courtesy of Author

Now that you know how to create a few patterns on your own, how about we check out the difference between Zentangle and doodling? That way you know when you're creating one on your own and when you're not.

Chapter Six – The Difference between Doodling and Zentangling

People will often confuse Zentangling with doodling and say that they've doodled all their lives and never knew that it had a term. However, Zentangling is far different from doodling, even if the outcomes can look the same. There are some major differences between the two.

When you Zentangle, you're not just aimlessly doodling a picture. Each press of the pen against the paper, each stroke to make a pattern, is meant to beget peace and calmness in your mind. There is no foundation for the drawing that you're creating; there is just the pattern that your mind creates as you go along. Therefore, a Zentangle rarely comes out looking like an actual object such as an animal or a scene.

It's a form of meditation that uses art and a specific method of deliberate intentions that creates a non-objective drawing made of tangles or patterns, and it can be viewed from all four sides without prejudice. Zentangle is more about the process rather than the outcome.

There is no right side up to a Zentangle because it should not contain a recognizable object. It's a focused, mindful process whereas doodling is something that you do with your hands while your mind is idly thinking about something else. It's easy to confuse the two outcomes of Zentangle and doodling, but the processes are very different.

It's imperative to remember that a tangle does not represent any natural or actual figure, object, or scene. A pattern is not always a tangle. We already discussed what makes a tangle in Chapter Four, but if you need a refresher, remember that a tangle is only two or three strokes, is non-representational, and does not use any mechanics such as a ruler to guide the pattern.

While you're perusing the internet for Zentangle ideas and art, keep in mind what you're looking at. You'll be able to recognize a Zentangle because it will have deliberate strokes and it will have been done with thought. Doodles are thoughtless and will often be representational of something in some way, but Zentangles are more about the following of the pattern, and usually come out very intricate. Someone who is Zentangling is tuning in to what they're doing rather than tuning out, and this shows in their Zentangles.

A Zentangler forgets about their worries as they're focusing on the pen strokes. Another giveaway when it comes to Zentangles is that the strings will fade away into the pattern. Those who don't know what they are doing will draw their strings in dark pen.

Remember that Zentangle is never about the finished product but about the process.

Chapter Seven – The Standard Value Patterns and Curves

There are six different standard patterns and curves that go along with Zentangling. You can use these patterns and curves in order to brighten up your Zentangle. Let's go over the six most common patterns and curves you'll see in a Zentangle, and then we'll take a look at some more intricate patterns you can try out in the following chapter.

Aura

The aura enhancement or pattern is perhaps one of the easiest to do as it's simply tracing around a pattern you've already drawn to give it a glowing effect. Drawing an aura around an existing pattern is a great example of how to Zentangle because there is no need to figure out where to draw the next line, you're just tracing what is already existent, and you can't tell what the shape of the next one is going to look like, so you continue to draw the one you're currently drawing.

It's a basic component to many different Zentangles and that's why those who are just beginning should try to incorporate auras into their drawings. It's a wonderful way to learn how to be aware of the pen strokes, the control of your pen, and how to focus on what you're doing in the present. Drawing auras also reminds the Zentangler to rotate their tile as they are drawing and teaches them that the pattern is able to be viewed from anywhere rather than just one side.

Some ideas to dress up your auras might be to Zentangle the space that's between the auras, or to change up the auras as you go along to make them all unique.

An example of an aura is as follows.

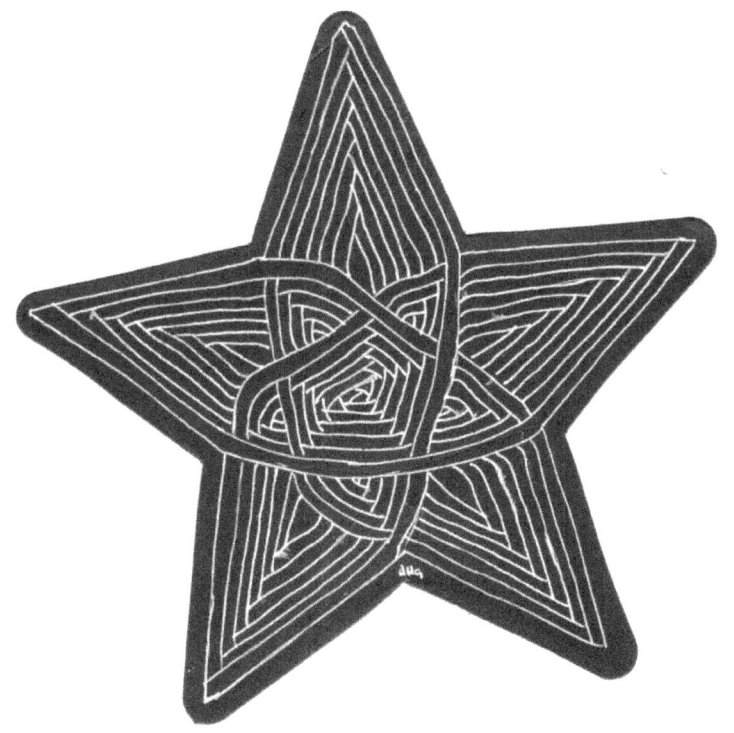

Photo courtesy of Heather Gladden at Flickr.com

Perfs

Perfs are a great addition to any Zentangle, but they seem to do best when used as a border against an existing pattern. Perfs are tiny, round circles or bubbles that can be used on their own or they can be placed around the edges of tangles, patterns, and even on a string as their own, standalone pattern.

Perfs are a great way for beginners to add a unique twist to their Zentangle without having to strain for ideas. Creating these small circles and bubbles inside and outside of patterns adds flare and it really helps the Zentangler get into the zone of creating the repetitive patterns and concentrating on what they're doing. There really isn't a wrong way to use perfs!

An example of perfs is as follows. The red arrow pointing to the small dots between the two strings is pointing out the perfs.

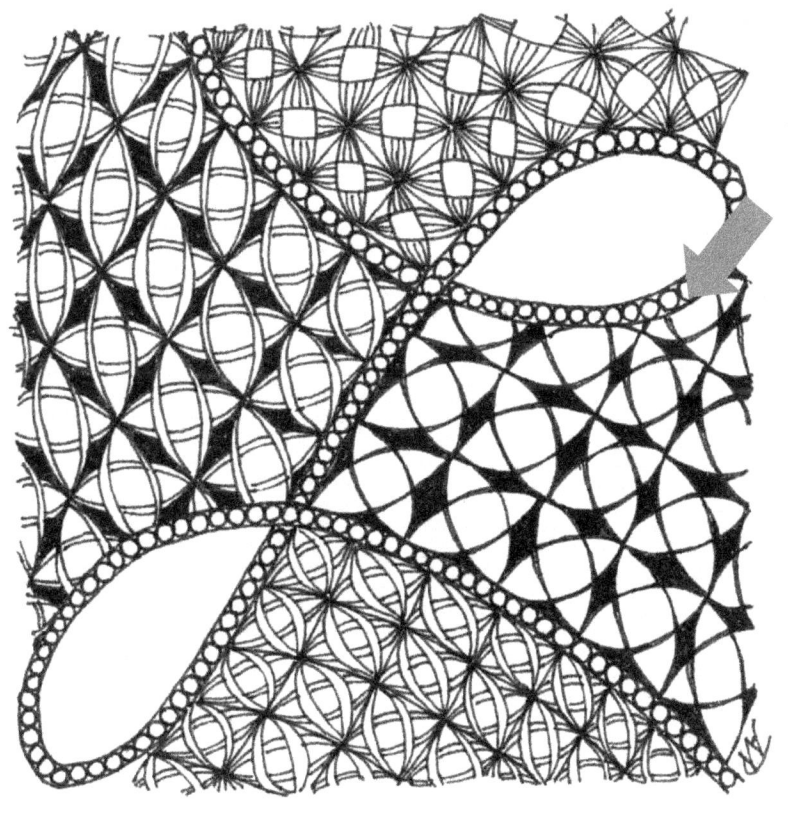

Photo courtesy of terem13 at Flickr.com

Dewdrop

The dewdrop is actually a string rather than a pattern, but it's incorporated into a pattern to give it a three-dimensional effect. In order to create a dewdrop, create a string that is a circle inside of the square string that is the border of the Zentangle. Then draw a simple pattern inside of that string, and draw it rather large. When you continue the pattern on the outside of the string, you can create a new pattern completely or you can repeat the pattern inside the circular string, only much smaller. This almost looks like a magnifying effect.

Here's an example of a dewdrop string at work.

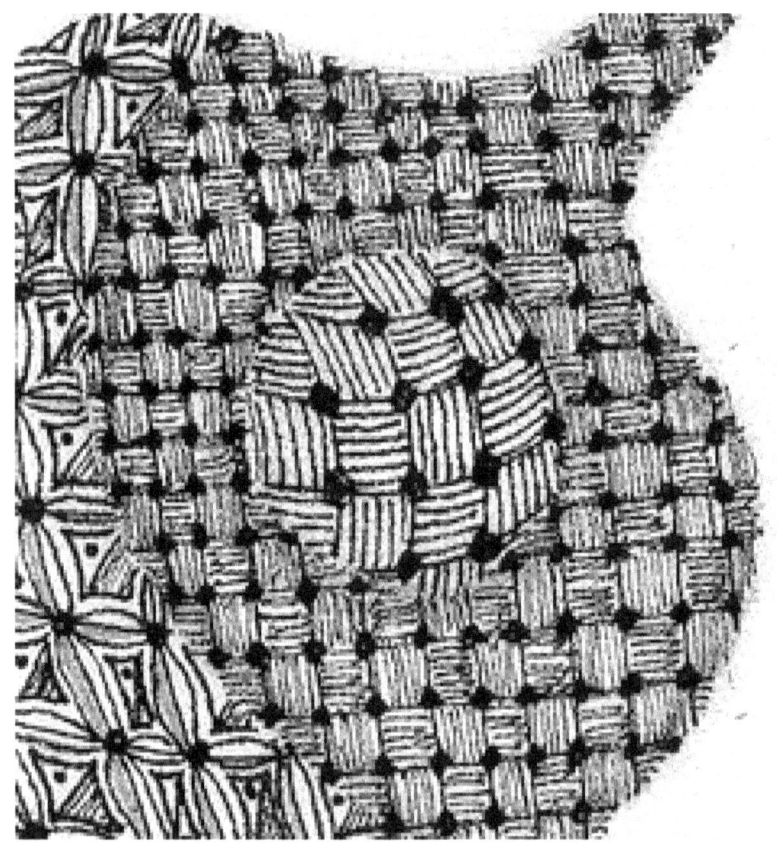

Photo courtesy of Jella at Flickr.com

Shading

Shading may not really be a string or a pattern, but it's definitely something that someone who is familiar with the concept can attempt, or even someone who's new to it! Remember that Zentangling is all about the process and not about the end result, so if shading feels comforting and relaxing for you, then by all means add it to your design!

Here's a great example of how you can easily use shading to add some depth to your project.

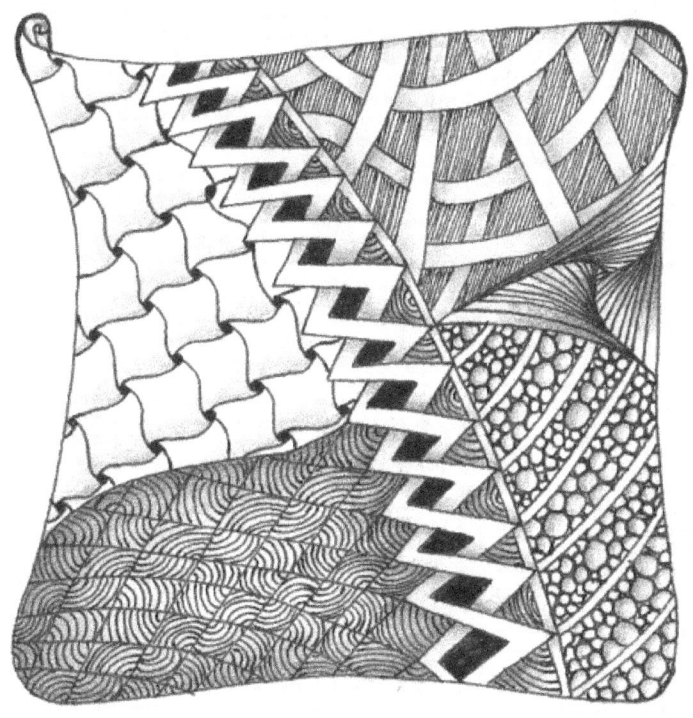

Photo courtesy of Vinyleraser at Flickr.com

Rounding

Rounding is the act of connecting together the ends of a rounded pattern and shading in the connections. A good example of this is as follows.

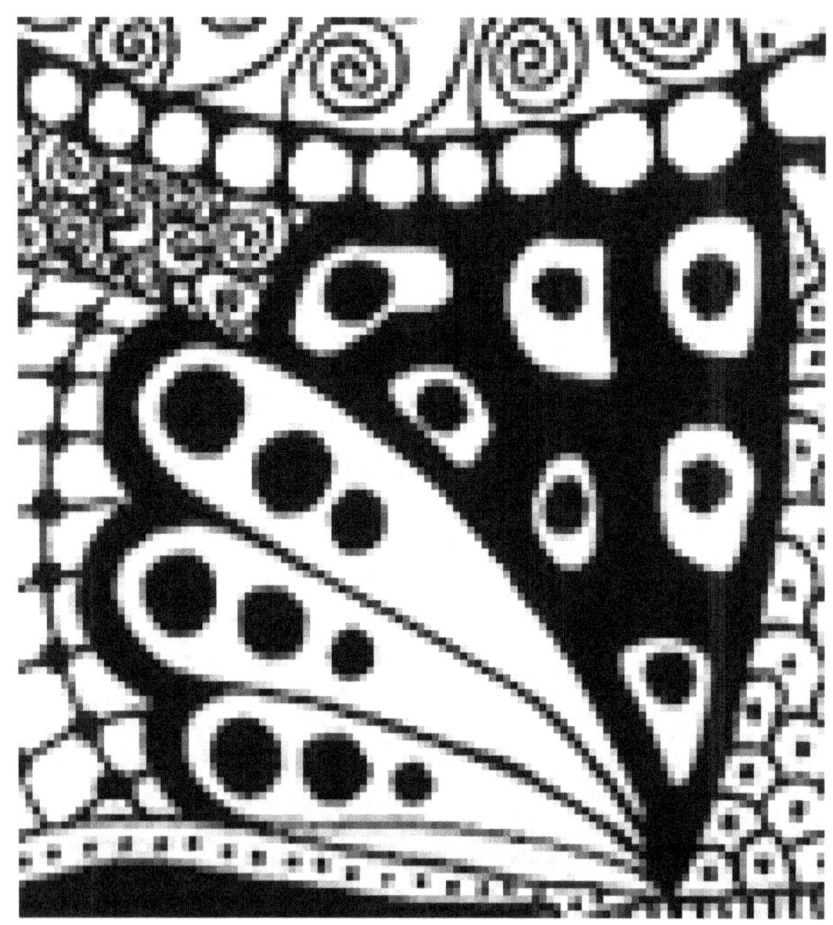

Photo courtesy of PRalle at Flickr.com

Sparkle

Sparkle looks pretty easy, but it's actually a little more involved than some of the other pattern enhancements.

Sparkle is like an aura, but there is a gap on either end of each line so that the aura looks like it's sparkling. Therefore, sparkle is a pattern enhancement that someone who really wants to learn to focus and concentrate as they're Zentangling should attempt.

A good example of what sparkle looks like is as follows.

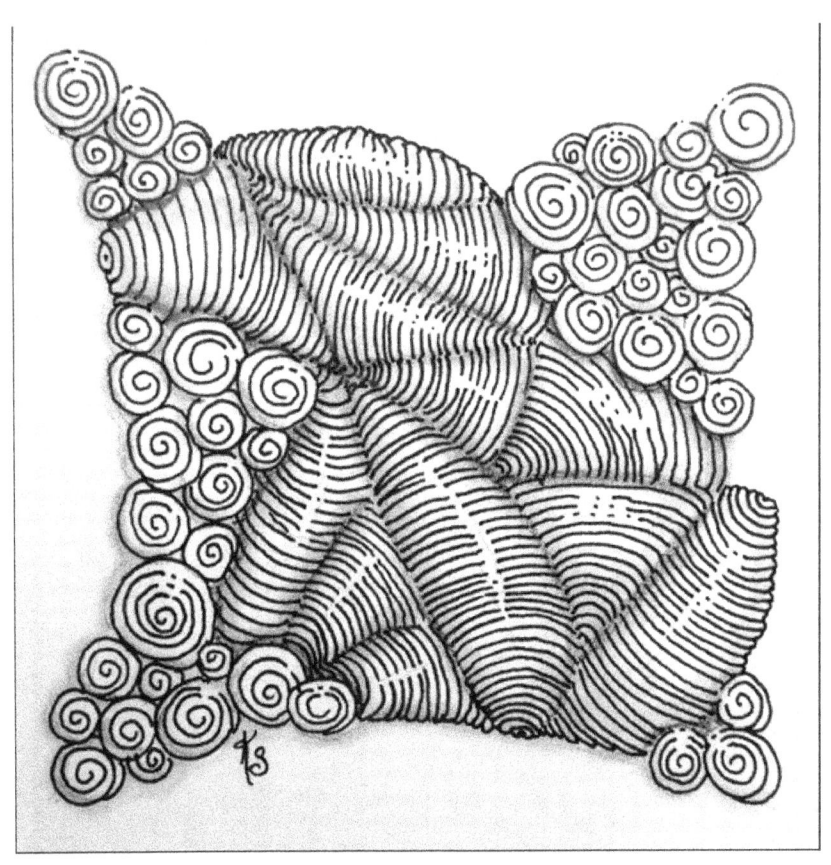

Photo courtesy of Kurki15 at Flickr.com

Points and Curves

This is a really fun pattern that a beginner can use in order to hone their concentration and focus so that they remain in the present. Remember, you want to choose patterns that are not too easy; otherwise, you lose the point of concentration and being in the present while you Zentangle.

The steps to draw this pattern are as follows:

1. Draw a triangle on your tile, but leave three gaps, one on either side as such:

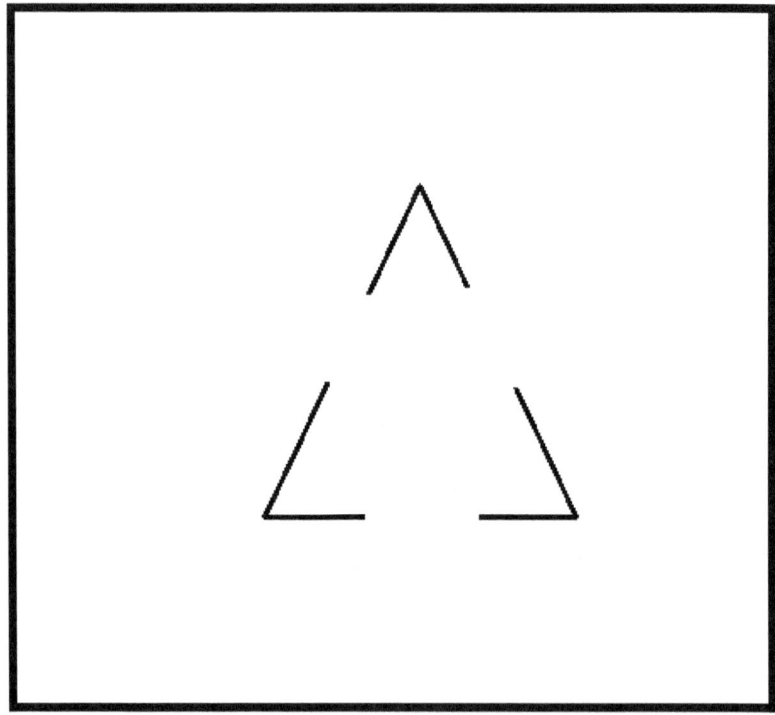

Photo courtesy of Author

2. Now draw little Pacman figures with their mouths open facing the openings of the triangle, like this:

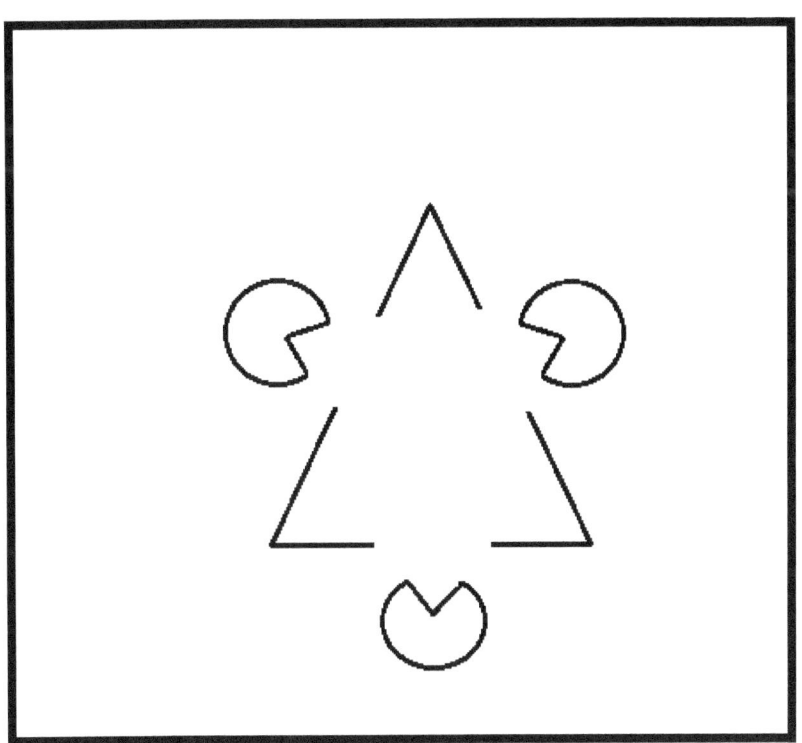

Photo courtesy of Author

3. Now shade in the little Pacman figures like this:

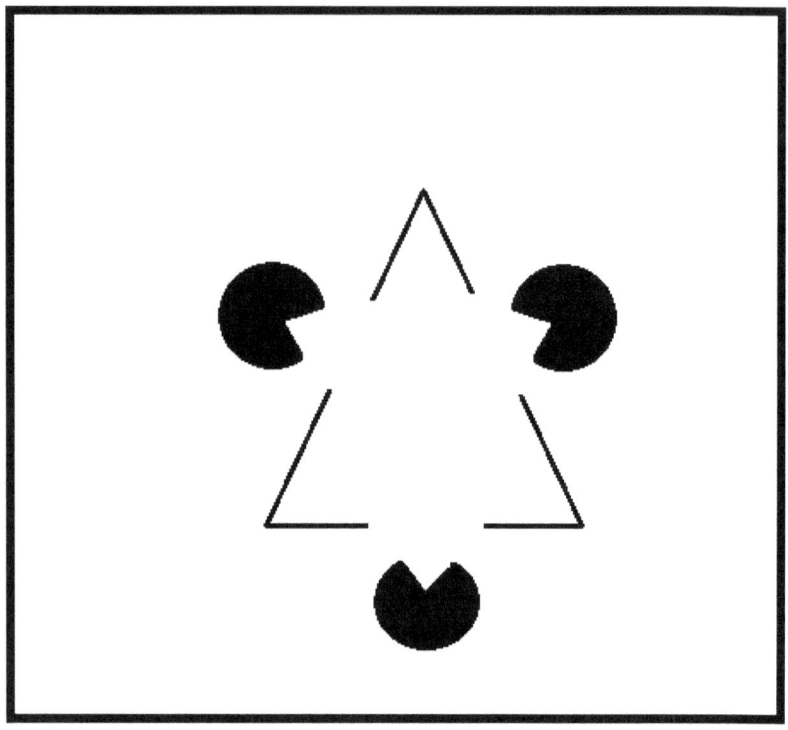

Photo courtesy of Author

You can replicate this pattern at different angles on the same tile or you can add some sparkles to it to make it more interesting. Some have even decided to put a tangle inside of the triangle part of this pattern. As long as you do not forget the main focus of Zentangle, you can do whatever you want with your pattern!

Chapter Eight – Creating Depth

When you want to create depth with your Zentangle, you can do it in many different ways. There's the three-dimensional option we discussed in the previous chapter with the dewdrop, or you can make your entire Zentangle round and make the pattern go from large in the center to small on the outer rims or vice versa to make it look like you're going down a tunnel. You can shade in certain areas of the Zentangle to make it stand out, and to make it look different from every angle. There are so many different ways that you can create depth with a Zentangle, so I'm going to discuss some of the most popular ones in this chapter. I encourage you to go out and look at many pictures of Zentangles to see what you can do with yours.

Shading

Perhaps the easiest way to create depth with a Zentangle is to shade in certain areas. For instance, if you want to highlight just one pattern on the tangle, then shade in the enclosed areas of that tangle. If you want to make a tangle's border stand out, then add some perfs and shade them in.

When you shade in a Zentangle, you can choose to use your pen and simply color in some of the different areas, or you can use a pencil. Now, the pencil is a nonstandard practice in the Zentangle world, but it's quickly becoming a highlight because it really brings out the Zentangles beautiful nature. You can use a 2B pencil to shade in your Zentangle to get that artistic look, or you can use a smudging tool to get a shaded appearance, too.

Here are some examples of shading that you can take a look at to get an idea of what you'd like to try out with your Zentangle. Remember that Zentangling is about the process, so take as much care shading as you did with drawing the actual pattern. You'll get the same benefits.

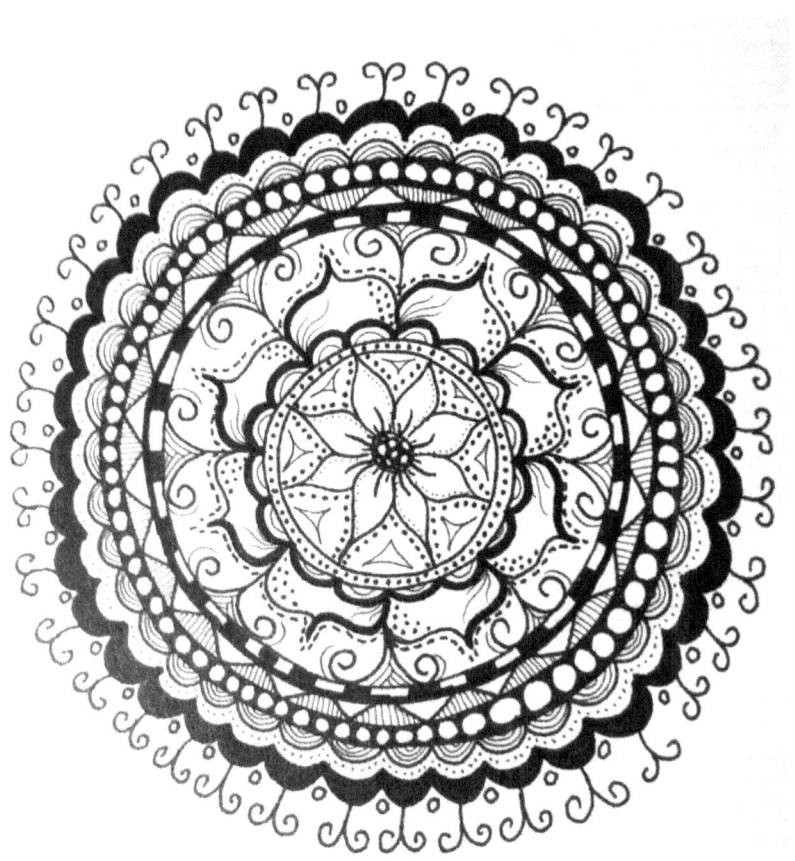

Photo courtesy of Persephone Pomegranate at Flickr.com

In this picture, you can see that the artist decided to shade in around the perfs, and some of their auras to create depth with their image. This is shading with a pen and not a pencil and doesn't really give the image a three-dimensional look. However, it is really beautiful and helps the different elements of the image stand out.

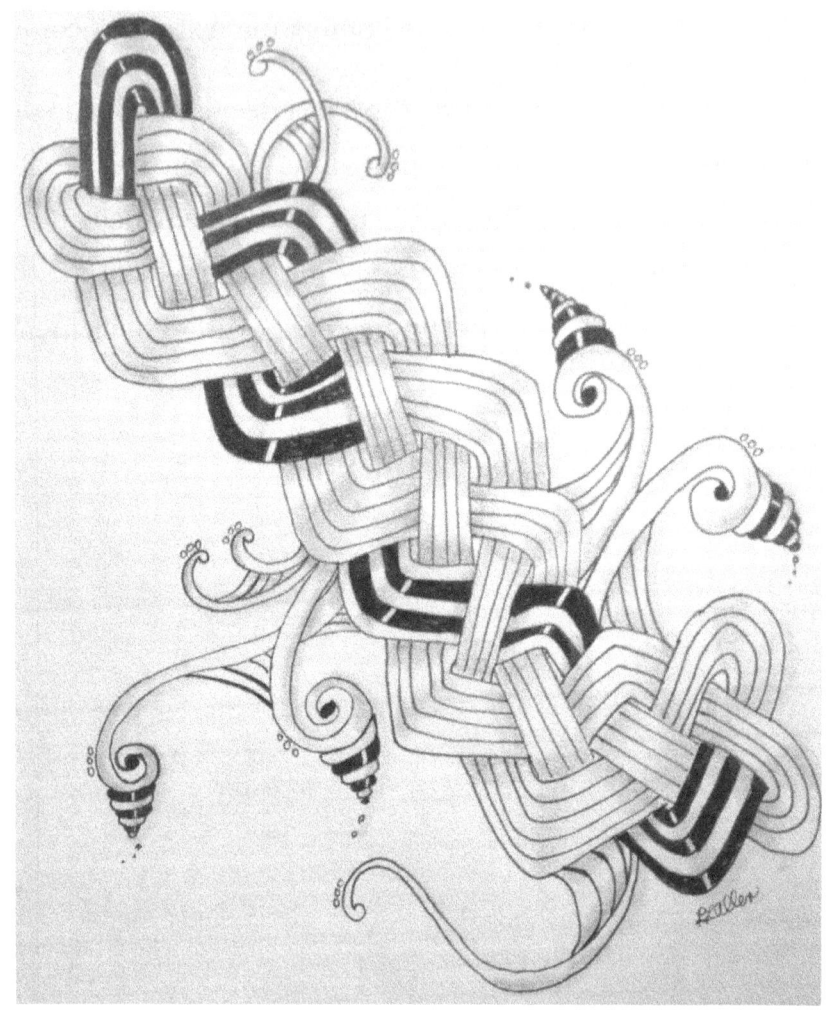

Photo courtesy of Lynn Allen at Flickr.com

In this image, you can see that both types of shading were involved in creating this Zentangle. The solid black areas were shaded in with a pen to make a few of the bands of the tangle stand out, and areas where the lines appear to curve have been shaded with a bit of pencil or a smearing motion. This gives the tangle an almost three-dimensional look as if it's truly pieces of fabric or rope intertwined with one another.

Three Dimensional Looks

There are several different ways to make a Zentangle look three dimensional. One of them was already discussed, shading, but shading only goes so far. If you want a truly three-dimensional look, I suggest you start out with the dew drop method mentioned in the previous chapter.

Then you can move on to the method of overlapping that makes it look like this.

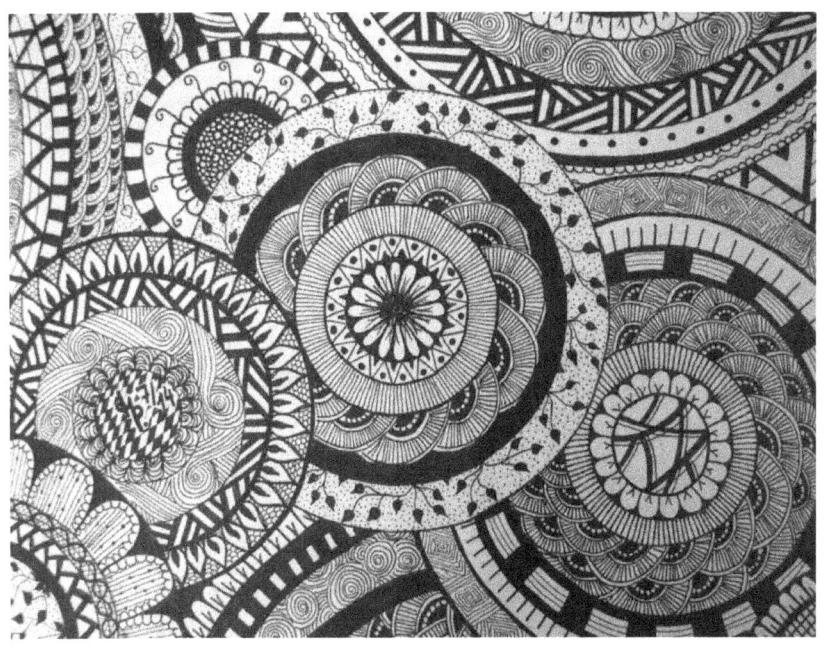

Photo courtesy of Semkyi at Flickr.com

You can also use this method that makes it look like the pattern is spiraling down. First you have to draw a spiral, and then fill in the pattern, and get smaller with the pattern as you go down the spiral, like this.

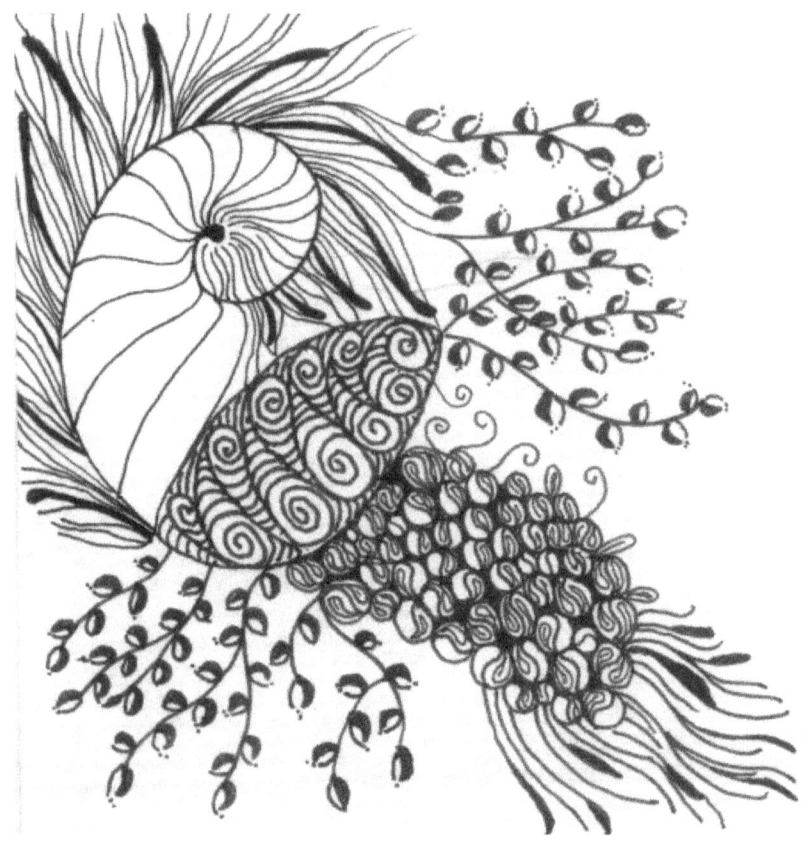

Photo courtesy of Tricia J at Flickr.com

There are many different ways to make your Zentangle pop. These are the two most utilized methods, but there are some intricate designs that you can use in order to make your

Zentangle stick out from the rest. We're going to discuss those in the next chapter.

Chapter Nine – Intricate Designs

There are so many patterns that you can choose from to create a tangle, and there are many different patterns just waiting to be discovered.

In the following picture, you'll see that the shape of your tangle does not have to be a square. You can draw the square border, and create any shape string that you wish in order to create a perfect design! Don't be limited by the box, but *embrace* it.

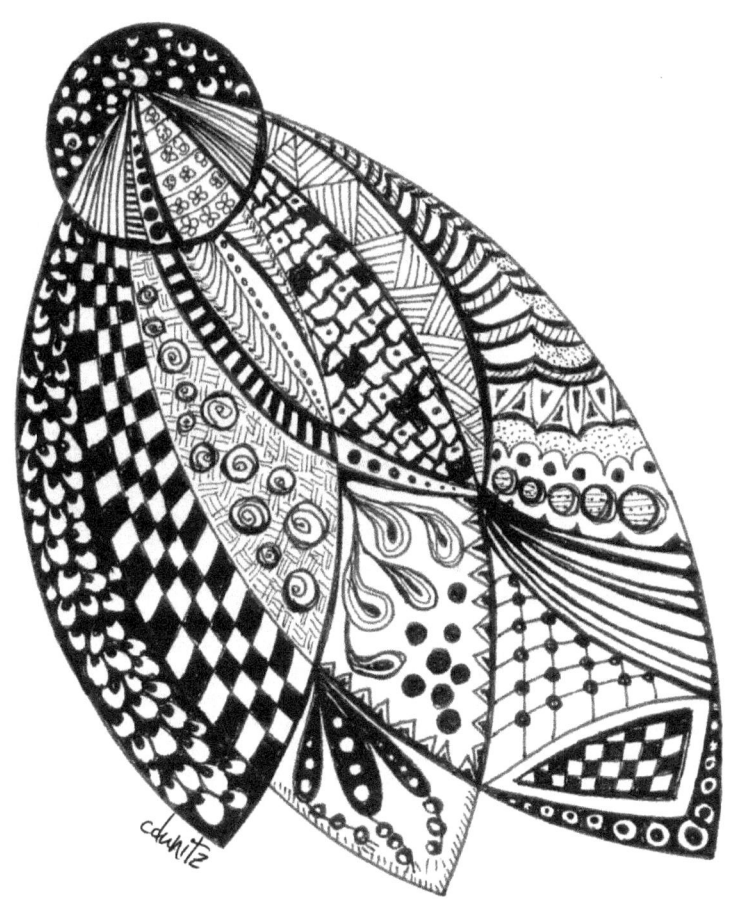

Photo courtesy of Claudia Brooke at Flickr.com

Another great way to make your Zentangle more intricate is to make a design within a doodle. Most purists of the art would consider this not a Zentangle, but it will definitely give your picture a new edge! Take a look at this Zentangle that uses strings that created the shape of a cat and then Zentangled the interior spaces.

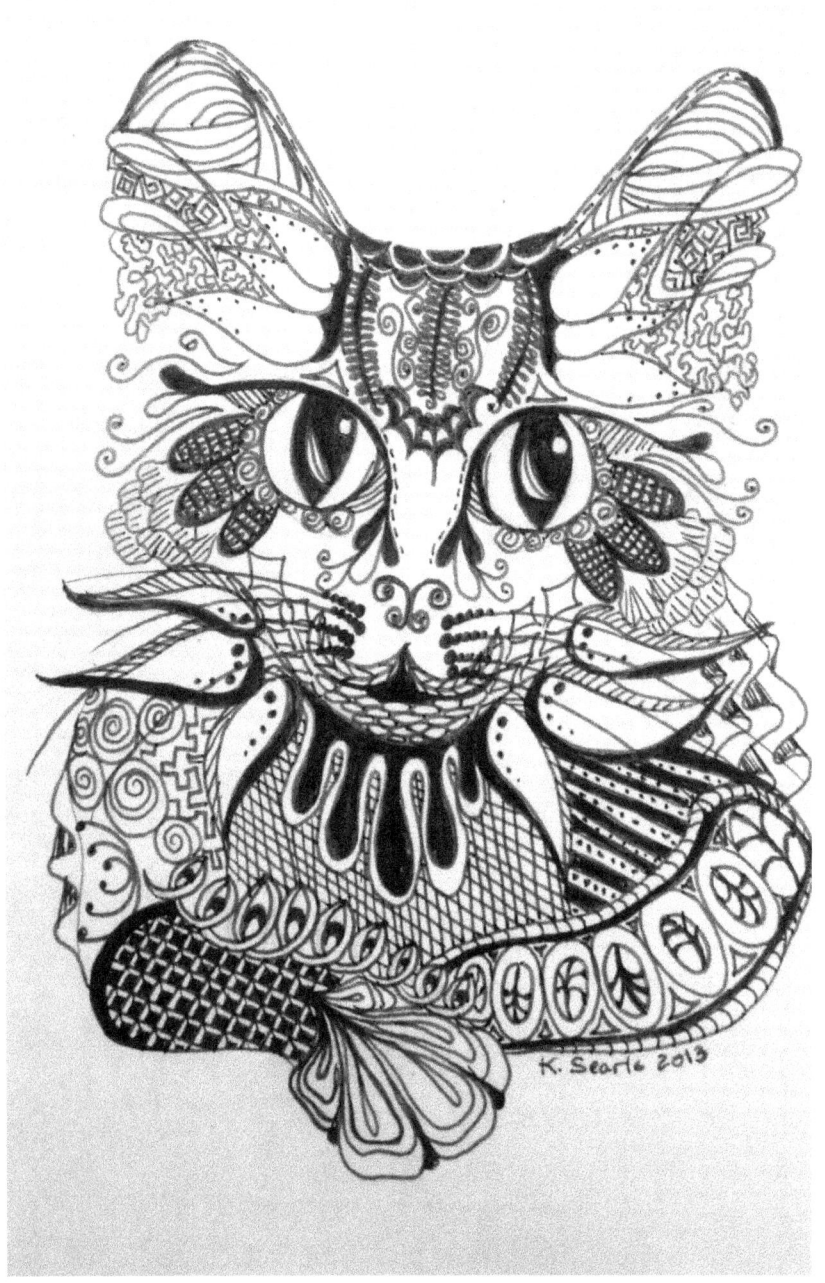

Photo courtesy of Kari at Flickr.com

When it comes to creating a Zentangle, remember that all of the tangles are intricate and involved for a reason. They're meant to take you away from your troubled thoughts about the past and the future, and allow your mind to relax while you remain in the present and focused on your task. Zentangles can be as intricate or as easy as you please, just as long as you are getting the benefits from drawing them.

Let's take a look at how you can add color, Zentangle on fabric and find support for Zentangle online in the next chapter.

Chapter Ten – Adding Color, Zentangling on Fabric, and Zentangling Support

I'm going to discuss methods of Zentangling that are not approved by the creators of this meditation and art form. The original founders of this method of relaxation do not use colors because they believe the method is much more beneficial if the artist is not focused on the different colors that can be added to the tangle. This adds in active thinking that draws away from the meditative aspects of the drawing. However, adding color and Zentangling on other mediums is definitely becoming more and more popular, so I feel there is a need to discuss how you can do this if you'd like to learn.

Zentangling with Color

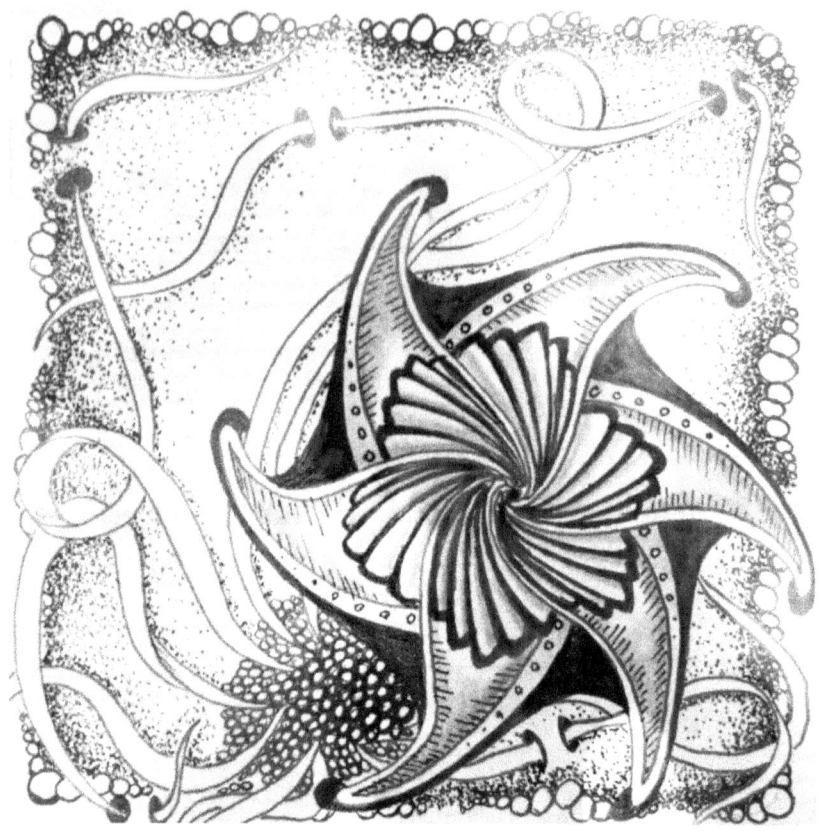

Photo courtesy of Sarah Nesthelde at Flickr.com

As you can see in the previous picture, Zentangling with color can really make an image pop out and gives it a lot of depth. Depending on the colors you use, you could make your Zentangle seem moody and fickle, or you can use some brighter colors and make it feel cheery and joyful, like in the following picture.

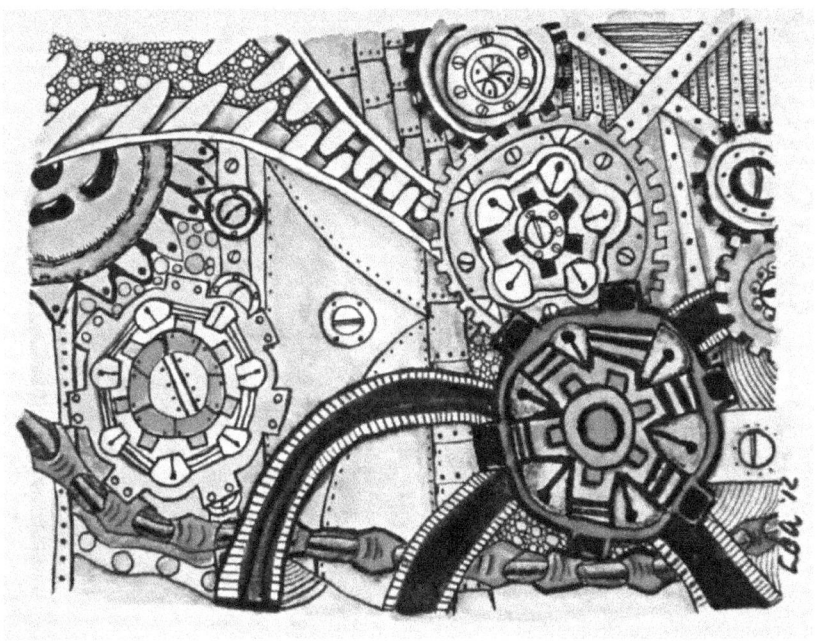

Photo courtesy of Lea Cook at Flickr.com

A more classy way of adding color to a Zentangle is to use one color that just highlights a few aspects of the Zentangle, like so.

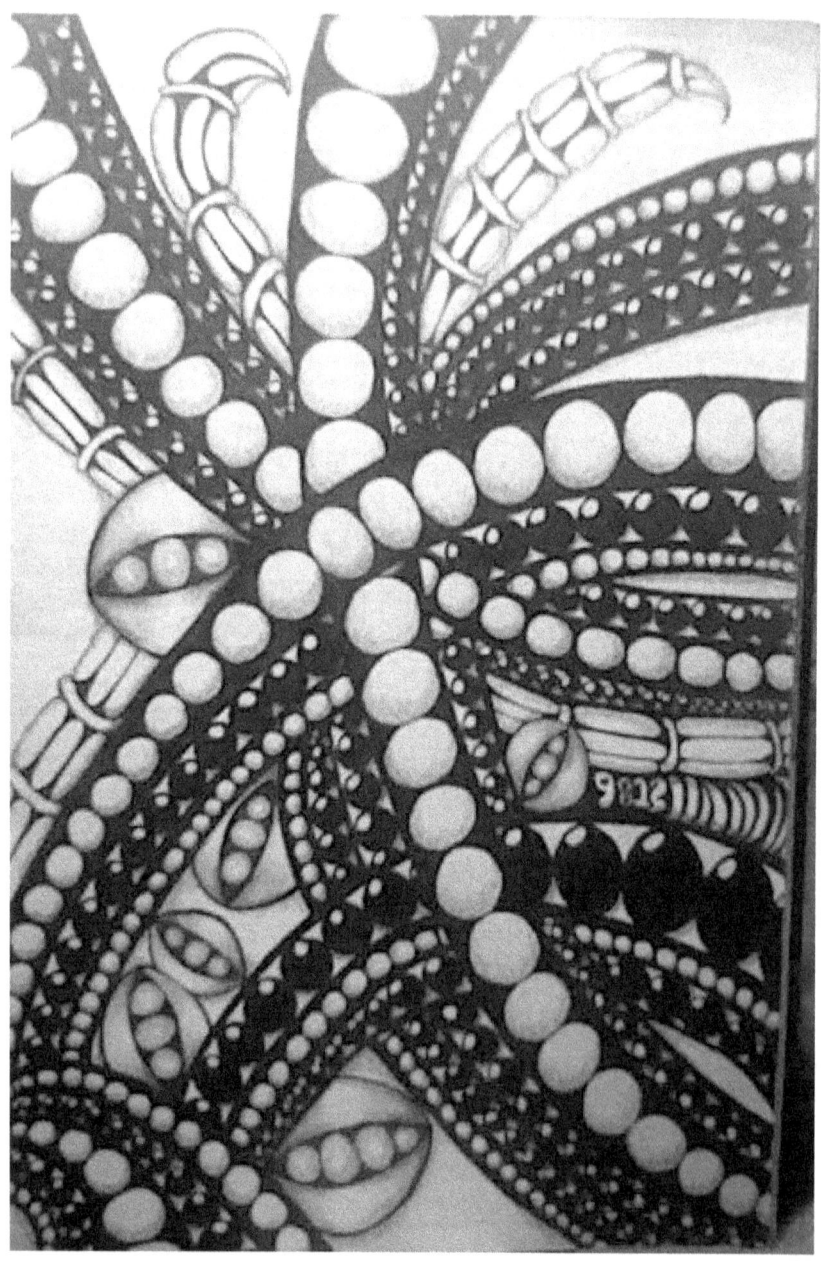

Photo courtesy of Grammacozy62 at Flickr.com

Zentangling on Fabric

There are many different ways to Zentangle on fabric. You can use a special paint, use different colored yarns to make a Zentangle pattern while knitting, and even sew different pieces of fabric together to make a Zentangle pattern. Some even use different colored threads to create a pattern that sewn onto one piece of fabric. Zentangling on fabric is a relatively new practice, but creating patterns with fabric and thread is not. It takes a bit more practice to learn the techniques, but the rewards are definitely worth it!

Take a look at some amazing ideas on how to use Zentangle to make beautiful pattern pieces.

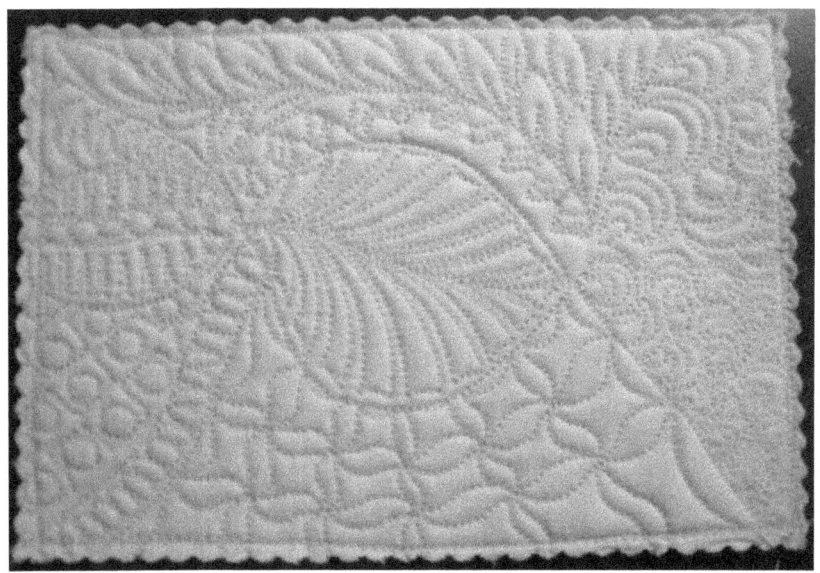

Photo courtesy of Becky Knopp at Flickr.com

The artist used thread to create her Zentangle artwork.

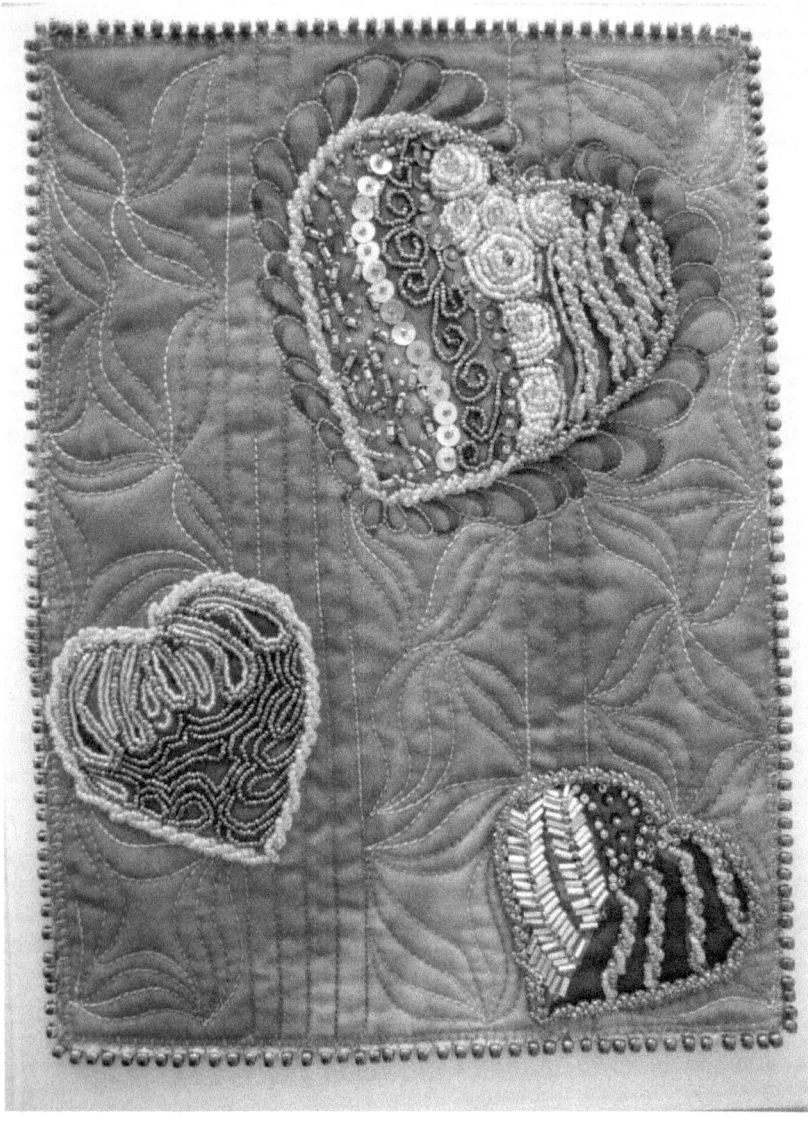

Photo courtesy of Robbie Payne at Flickr.com

This artist used fabric, thread, and beads to create their Zentangle patterns!

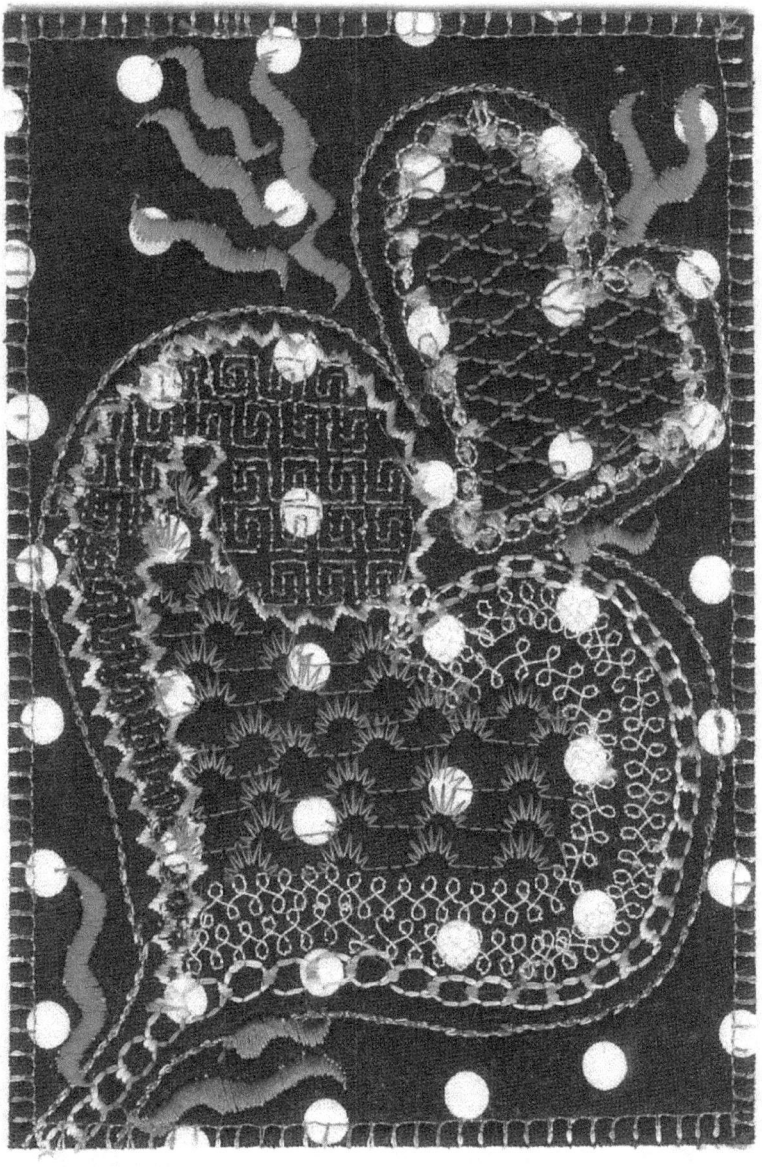

Photo courtesy of shereesews at Flickr.com

This postcard was created by using a piece of fabric and some thread to make the designs. This is a very intricate, unique piece of art that most likely took some time to create.

Zentangling on Other Mediums

There are numerous different mediums out there to use when you want to Zentangle. Many executives have been caught Zentangling on their coffee cups in the morning, or on the morning newspaper when they're finished reading the highlights. Zentangling can be done anywhere with anything! Don't limit yourself to that square piece of paper and a pen unless you want to. Allowing your creativity to flow and being in the moment with it is what Zentangle is all about, so try to think outside the box for your next project!

Support

There are numerous websites out there that can help you with Zentangling. Simply go online and research Zentangle on a search engine, and you'll find hundreds of results. If you want to take a look at the patterns that you can choose from, try this website: https://www.zentangle.com/. Or look on some more popular websites like Pinterest or Flickr for some more Zentangle ideas!

There are also workshops and classes that you can take both online or offline, so if you want to get the full experience of Zentangle, I suggest you try out a few of their classes. The original founders of the practice actually hold their own classes and are willing to answer questions for those who are looking to get in-depth with the practice.

Conclusion

I know there is a lot to take in about the art of Zentangle in this book, but I urge you to grab the few tools you do need to get started and try it out for yourself. The important part is actually *starting* the Zentangle and following through with it. You can read about it all day and look at pictures for ideas for hours, but you'll only benefit from the practice by actually doing it. Zentangle is all about meditation and being in the present moment; don't forget that important aspect of the art.

So your first step after reading this book is to sit down with a piece of white paper and a black pen. Draw a box, create a string or a series of strings inside the box, and start drawing repetitive patterns! Remember to incorporate any mistakes into the pattern so that it looks natural rather than trying to get rid of that mistake. There are many mistakes that have grown into something truly amazing and beautiful.

I hope you enjoyed this eBook on how to Zentangle! If you did, please leave a review at your online eBook retailer's website.

Thank you for reading!

If you enjoyed the information in this book, please go to your online eBook provider and leave a positive review. It would be greatly appreciated.

Thank you for reading!

Dear Reader,

I would like to invite you to join my email list! This way you will never miss a new release, and even get new Kindle books for FREE – because we will drop you a line when they are on free promotion on Amazon!

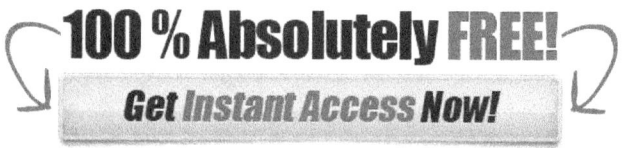

Click here to get instant access to all our FREE books now!

(Click the link or enter http://bit.ly/19eWRoW into your browser.)